TESTIMONALS

"Patrisha is living proof that no matter how bad of a "hand you are dealt" at birth, you can rise like a phoenix from the ashes without blame or resentment to live an aware, fullfilling, healthy and happy life."

John Douillard
Author of *Body, Mind and Sport* and *The 3-Season Diet*

"Your book has directed me to deal with the reality of life. By telling the details of your own life and how you made the transition from the tough side of society to the gifted and inspiring side, you lead me in the right direction. You have taken yourself from the dark side of existence up to the illuminated vision of our multidimensional world, and you have gathered new understanding of life as given by God himself. Your book tells me how I can direct myself in the same way. I have needed a deeper and more meaningful understanding of life and in your book you have explained the direction I need to follow in order to deal with life in this world the right way."

Andrew Milner, Film Industry Executive, Los Angeles, CA.

"This book guides the reader into the necessary spiritual practices to affect a great healing. A must read for anyone on the recovery path."

Ron Russell, CEO of Midwest Research,
and artist of *Crop Circles Calendar* series by Llewllyn.

Transforming Darkness into Light

A Guidebook for Spiritual Seekers

PATRISHA RICHARDSON

PLEASE NOTE THAT TRANSFORMING DARKNESS INTO LIGHT REPRESENTS THE PERSONAL EXPERIENCE AND TEACHINGS OF THE AUTHOR. THE INFORMATION IS NOT TO BE TAKEN AS MEDICAL ADVICE. IF YOU PRACTICE ANY OF THE EXERCISES OR SUGGESTIONS IN THIS BOOK, DO SO AFTER CONSULTING WITH YOUR PHYSICIAN OR OTHER HEALTH CARE PRACTICIONER. THE AUTHOR OFFERS NO GUARANTEE THAT HEALING OR PERMANENT CHANGE WILL OCCUR.

THE INSTRUCTIONS FOR HYPNOTHERAPY SESSIONS (E.G. PAST LIFE REGRESSION) WRITTEN IN THIS BOOK ARE INCLUDED FOR THE USE OF LICENSED PRACTITIONERS IN HYPNOSIS. IT IS RECOMMENDED THAT ALL NON-LICENSED READERS SEEK THE ADVICE OF A PROFESSIONAL AND DO NOT ATTEMPT TO APPLY THE HYPNOTHERAPY TECHNIQUES ON ANY OTHER PERSON THAN SELF.

Copyright (c) 2000 Patrisha Richardson
This book is copyrighted. All rights reserved. No part of this book may be reproduced in any form or by any means without permission in writing from the author, except for brief excerpts quoted in published reviews of the book.

ISBN: 0-615-11385-0

Manufactured in the United States of America
Set in Caxton and Times

Published by Absolute Truth Publications
patrisharich@aol.com - 1-800-484-9777 code 1594
www.absolutetruthpublications.com

Editorial services by Charol Messenger, Messenger Literary Services, e-mail CharolM@aol.com; and Jean Rita Linder

Printing Services by United Graphics Inc. GordonUGI@aol.com

Design and Cover Art by Li Hertzi, LiHertzi Design,
e-mail lihertzi@mindspring.com

ACKNOWLEDGEMENTS

I would like to thank all the people who contributed to the writing and production of this book. First and foremost I thank Jean Linder from the bottom of my heart for helping me write, edit, and proof the text, and for being here to support me all hours of the day. I thank B.G. Stivers for encouraging me to write the book and for preliminary help with the writing. Stacey Nielsen helped write "Patrisha's Story."

Many people contributed to the production of the book. Charol Messenger provided editing, proofing services, support, and much time on the phone. Cindy Danielson helped with the proofing, and Gar Bergstedt lovingly helped me with the technical aspect of the computer. Christine Testolini of The Integrity Agency offered me consultation services regarding book publishing and marketing. Li Hertzi did the layout and incredible cover art.

For personal support I would like to thank my son, Kol Richardson, and my partner-in-love, Paul McLean. They endured my continual focus on the book for the past year and offered constant encouragement. I am very grateful to Bill and Jean Worley for their support. I am also deeply grateful to all of my friends and the light workers who have encouraged, loved, and supported me through the years.

I especially want to thank in advance all those who will use the techniques in this book to improve their lives and contribute to the enlightenment of the planet.

This book is dedicated to my Spiritual Masters

FORWARD

I first met Patrisha Richardson a decade ago, in March 1990, and I still honor that day as one of the most important landmarks of my life. I had recently awakened to metaphysics and wanted to meet a "psychic." The friend who recommended Patrisha to me said, "She does do psychic readings, but more importantly, she uses her intuitive gifts to help you resolve issues in your life. You will make better use of her time and expertise if you have something you'd like to work on." So, somewhat as a lark, I decided to ask her to help me resolve my chronic depression. I had no idea that when I sat across from Patrisha in her healing room and asked to work on depression, I was about to be catapulted into the world of spirit and spiritual healing. She took one look at my aura, pulled out her poster depicting the higher self, and said to this depressed, reclusive atheist, "Hang onto your hat, girl. You are going back to God!" Who me? Yes, me.

Over the years I have done more than sixty counseling sessions with Patrisha. We used the techniques presented in this book, especially the mind-clearing techniques in chapter five and past-life regression in chapter four to delve into the "can of worms" of my current and past-life issues. I don't think we left a single stone unturned. To say the work is powerful and life-changing is almost an understatement.

When I first met Patrisha, she taught these techniques in a ten-week course. I took it twice. I then was able to use these techniques on myself and to facilitate others. In 1992, Patrisha invited me to be an apprentice. For five years, with the client's permission, I witnessed the client's verbal session with Patrisha and then did a hand-on healing

Forward

on him/her using many of the healing techniques in chapter three. So, I not only personally experienced the impact of these techniques on myself, I witnessed changes and growth in literally hundreds of others. I continue to be in awe of this body of work.

The underlying theme in Patrisha's work and teachings is spiritual growth as part of the path of enlightenment and ascension. All of the mental, emotional, and physical healing definitely improves our day-to-day lives. More importantly, it clears the decks for expansion of consciousness, increased contact with spirit, and anchoring more light onto the planet. I have personally experienced and witnessed the initiation ceremonies presented in chapter nine, "Ascension." This chapter is closest to my heart. These major infusions of light and leaps in growth have become the cornerstone of my life. They are sacred events. Every few years when Patrisha and I sense I am ready for another initiation ceremony, I am as thrilled as most women are at the prospect of their wedding day.

Patrisha is more than just a facilitator for the growth of others. As you will see in "Patrisha's Story," she is also a human being pursuing her own path of growth and enlightenment. And she is doing so against enormous odds. "Transforming Darkness to Light" is such an apt title for her book. Her roots in a dysfunctional, addiction-ridden, violent family led to personal struggles with alcohol, drugs, violence, and crime. That she even survived is astonishing. That she escaped the darkness and began a successful recovery process is truly inspirational. That she became a healer, teacher, and facilitator of enlightenment falls into the category of miracles.

The spiritual path is not easy. Most of the time it isn't much fun. The path to peace and joy is well worth the effort, but it takes an incredible amount of hard work, determination, and discipline. It can be incredibly painful to revisit and (re)experience all the painful events and traumas of our lives as we resolve and clear stuck emotions, limiting beliefs, and physical disorders. Each time I sit on the "pity-pot" (more often than I care to admit), and am finally ready to climb off, I think of Patrisha. We both "awoke" spiritually around the age of thirty-eight. But there is nothing in the first decades of my life that even remotely compares to the traumas and challenges she has faced and surmounted. And, if she can face those enormous odds, and thrive, then so can I. And so can you.

The image of her courage, plus the obvious power of her indomitable spirit, begins to push me off the pity-pot. I usually complete the dismount by counting my blessings. And, again, I turn to the image of Patrisha. Anytime I feel betrayed, abandoned, or dumped-on by spirit, I remember the gift of Patrisha and I feel blessed. I am enormously grateful to her personally and professionally. Many, many people are. And, once you read this book and use the techniques for your own recovery and growth, you too can share in that blessing and gratitude.

Jean Rita Linder

Denver, Colorado

April, 2000

TABLE OF CONTENTS

PATRISHA'S STORY	1
INTRODUCTION	33

CHAPTER 1
ACCESSING INFORMATION AND
DEVELOPING YOUR INTUITIVE GIFTS ... 37

INTUITIVE GIFTS	37
YOUR SPIRITUAL GUIDES	40
ACCESSING MESSAGES FROM SPIRIT	41
KINESIOLOGY OR MUSCLE TESTING	44
MUSCLE TESTING ANOTHER PERSON	45
MUSCLE TESTING YOURSELF	47
HOW TO DO AN INTUITIVE (PSYCHIC) READING	48

CHAPTER 2
SUBTLE BODIES AND CHAKRAS ... 53

SUBTLE BODIES	53
ETHERIC BODY	53
EMOTIONAL BODY	54
MENTAL BODY	55
SPIRITUAL BODY	55
CHAKRAS	56
FIRST CHAKRA	57
SECOND CHAKRA	58
THIRD CHAKRA	59
FOURTH CHAKRA	61
HIGH HEART CHAKRA	61

FIFTH CHAKRA	62
SIXTH CHAKRA	63
SEVENTH CHAKRA	63
NONPHYSICAL CHAKRAS	64

CHAPTER 3
HANDS-ON HEALING	**67**
IMPLANTS	69
COLOR HEALING	71
TONING	73
GROUNDING	74
GROUNDING TECHNIQUES	75
PROTECTION	76
PROTECTION TECHNIQUES	77
HOW NOT TO ABSORB OTHER PEOPLE'S NEGATIVITY	77
DEMONSTRATION OF HANDS-ON HEALING	79
ABSENTEE HEALING	86

CHAPTER 4
PAST LIVES	**93**
DEMONSTRATION OF PAST-LIFE REGRESSION	95
EXERCISE ONE	96
EXERCISE TWO	99

CHAPTER 5
MIND-CLEARING TECHNIQUES	**103**
MEDITATION	103

Table of Contents

Pattern Removal	106
Clearing Patterns	108
Pattern Removal Techniques	108
Symbology	112
Inner Child	115
Discovering Your Inner Child	115
Nurturing Your Inner Child to Learn Self-Love	116
Accessing and Nurturing Your Inner Child	117
Getting Answers From the Inner Child	119
Masculine-Feminine Balance	120
An Exercise to Balance Masculine and Feminine	124
Soul Retrieval	127
Soul Retrieval Technique	127
Removing Entities and Releasing Attachments	128
Entities	128
Disease Entities	130
Attachments	131
Technique for Releasing Attachments and Entities	132

Chapter 6
Other Ways to Improve the Quality of Your Life — 137

Creation and Manifestation	137
God Lives in the Mind	140
The Witness	141
Giving to Yourself First	143

TABLE OF CONTENTS

Youthing in the New Millennium	146
Exercise	147
Career Transitioning	149

Chapter 7
Extraterrestrials — **155**

Chapter 8
Kundalini — **159**
Kundalini Energy Healing	161
My Experiences with Kundalini	163
Kundalini - Myths, Fears, and Dangers	166
Some Examples of the Impacts of Kundalini	168
Nancy's Story	168
John's Story	169
Alan and Joanne's Story	169
Duane's Story	170
Kundalini Exercises	170
Guided Imagery	171
Kundalini Exercise One	171
Kundalini Exercise Two	172
Kundalini Exercise Three	172

Chapter 9
Ascension — **175**
| Guided Imagery | 180 |
| Lightbody | 181 |

TABLE OF CONTENTS

UNIFIED CHAKRA	184
INITIATIONS AND THE ENLIGHTENMENT PROCESS	186
FIRST AND SECOND INITIATIONS	188
THIRD INITIATION, THE BEGINNING OF SOUL-MERGE	189
PATRISHA'S PRE-SOUL-MERGE EXPERIENCE	192
PATRISHA'S SOUL-MERGE EXPERIENCE	192
FACILITATING A SOUL-MERGE INITIATION	193
FOURTH INITIATION	198
FACILITATING A FOURTH INITIATION CEREMONY	202
FIFTH INITIATION	203
FACILITATING A FIFTH INITIATION CEREMONY	205
SIXTH INITIATION	206
FACILITATING A SIXTH INITIATION CEREMONY	211
SEVENTH INITIATION AND ABOVE	213
ENLIGHTENMENT IS A PROCESS	214

Author's Note

Patrisha's Story is an autobiographical presentation of my personal struggle with drugs and alcohol. It is presented here as an example of one woman's successful transformation from darkness to light. The remainder of the book presents many of the teachings and techniques that have helped me and my clients in the recovery and spiritual growth process. It is not necessary to read Patrisha's Story to understand and benefit from the remainder of the book.

Patrisha's Story

*T*his particular lifetime has seemed like many lifetimes in one. I chose a very difficult astrological chart to live and learn by. I was destined to live on the streets most of my life, mainly by myself. From a very young age my intuition made a warrior-survivor out of me and for this I am truly grateful. I chose some very interesting parents to teach me - and abuse me - so I could take the hard and fast path to awareness and forgiveness, ultimately understanding that I am not really a victim of circumstances after all.

It has taken years of healing and recovery to peel off enough layers of armor so that I can be soft and feeling. It has taken years to reach a point where I can speak of my past history with detachment and without being triggered into self-pity or rage. I now feel sorrow for little Patti and sorry that she had to go through those experiences, yet I know that at a soul level I chose those experiences; and I am now grateful for this life opportunity to overcome the darkness and open to the light.

Patricia Suzanne O'Brien was born in Long Beach, California, December 22, 1944, at four thirty-five a.m. I was born into what would appear to be a normal, respectable, middle-class family. The goal was to "keep up with the Jones's," in line with the stereotypical 1940s and 1950s lifestyle. Mom and Dad went to the Presbyterian Church, sang in the choir, and elbowed up to the minister. This was the image they presented to the outside world. In our inner world we were a miserably dysfunctional family. My memories of those years are vivid. Both of my parents were addicted to drugs, alcohol, and gambling. After church Mom would go to the local bar to drink and flirt with men; while Dad spent the rest of the day with his girlfriend, or he went out drinking and gambling.

We moved constantly when I was growing up. Dad managed a chain of jewelry stores, and we had to move from city to city so he could turn failing businesses into profitable ones. Then we were off to the next jewelry store in the next city. I had no roots anywhere.

My sisters and I were the recipients of nightly whippings. Dad's nightly ritual was to pull off his skinny suede belt, snap it sadistically, and ask, "Who's first?" He took his anger out on all of us, but I happened to look most like my mother and he hated her, so this automatically made me the scapegoat. He screamed with flaming eyes, "I hate you, you whore! You stupid slut, you will never amount to anything!" Unfortunately I believed him, at least part of me did.

I would cry when he beat me, but I would also fight back. The others did not fight back like I did; consequently, I got beaten even harder. The first time I decided to rebel I laughed at him. This single moment of pride on my part became the beginning of real beatings. He used his fists and kicked me after that. One day I had an abscessed tooth and was in tremendous pain and immobilized in my room.

I was smoking a cigarette, trying to numb the pain, when Dad came in and started kicking me for smoking. The next day I went to school covered with bruises. The principal called my dad in and threatened to call the authorities if he ever saw bruises on me again. So, Dad found other ways to punish me.

There were other forms of abuse as well - emotional, mental, and spiritual. One of the family members said that Dad sexually abused her; she claims that he touched her inappropriately in bed. She and I slept together, so at some subconscious level I must have known something was going on. However, I don't have any definite proof that he sexually abused me. I do remember squirming around on his lap to avoid being grabbed and beaten at age seven. I thought sex might stop a beating. That approach came in handy in my later life.

My dad really tried to beat us down. His efforts succeeded with most of the family. However, I was the black sheep, the rebel. Not surprisingly, and much to my parents' dismay, I became a "wild and incorrigible" child. I was shipped from relative to relative. I was given many psychological tests, and my parents were always baffled when the results indicated there was nothing wrong with me and I was sent home again.

When I was eleven my parents divorced and I moved to Grand Junction, Colorado, with my mother. She was completely undisciplined. There were times when we didn't have food, heat, or light. We always had a good supply of candles, though, in case the lights were turned off. I was pretty grown up for my age and became the caretaker of my little sister.

School was tough for me. I was very unpopular because my mother managed to give our family a bad name due to her incessant love of men and their attention.

Another reason for my lack of popularity was my awful clothes. My only decent outfits were the ones I stole.

At Christmas when I was thirteen, my mom sauntered up to me, grabbed my hand, and slurred, "Come on, Patti, it's time to learn how to Christmas shop-lift." With one arm around me, and the other cradling her vodka, we ventured out together as mother and daughter to steal Christmas presents. In no time I learned how to stuff clothes, vodka, and anything within reach into my shirt and down my pants. The bottles of vodka fit best down the pants leg or in the crotch. Mother was so proud of me. This bonding experience brought us closer together and soon we were buddies, drinking buddies. She taught me to grow up in so many ways! We went to hillbilly bars. She put red lipstick on my lips and I wore my sister's bra stuffed with tissues to attract the men. We sat and drank, and I was lucky if I could find her at closing time. Occasionally I had to ride home with some cowboy, struggling to be sober enough to give coherent directions. This was pretty frightening for a thirteen-year-old.

At this time I began my personal battle with drugs and alcohol. It was easy. Mom worked in a pharmacy; every morning she popped Dexedrine (speed), and every night it was Nembutal (sleeping pills). She carried a purse full of pills - uppers and downers. I quickly got into the daily habit of reaching into Mom's purse and grabbing a handful of pills on my way to school.

I ran around in a Chicano gang during those years, which didn't help my reputation. We stood around a few blocks from school waiting for other female gang members to stroll by. Then we picked fights with them. One time I was silly enough to carry a double-edged razor blade in my bra. Someone told the school counselor about this and she was shocked, to say the least. "What about the possibility of cutting off your boob?" she asked. "Didn't you think about this?" This incident prompted a search of my locker and they found my daily stash of vodka in my lunch bucket. Didn't everybody take booze to the seventh grade every day?

One night I had a date with Jesse, one of the guys from the Chicano gang. I climbed out of my window to meet him, got in the car, and we drove to the peach orchards. Once we arrived three other guys who had been hiding under a blanket in the back seat made their presence known. They were not members of the gang, but Jesse had invited them along to gang-rape me. I was still a virgin then. Jesse stayed in the front seat while the three took turns holding me down in the back seat and tried to penetrate me. I screamed and tried to fight them off. They taunted me with comments such as, "Oh, she's really getting into this. She really likes it." Finally Jesse said, "That's enough," and made them stop. Although none of the guys fully penetrated me, when I got home there was blood on my white jeans. I could not tell my mother what had happened because I had snuck out.

For my fourteenth birthday I gave myself the birthday gift of having sex for the first time with a man I cared about. Although it hurt, I knew it was love. I'll never forget the back seat of that black 1938 Chevy, the musty smell of the fabric seats, and my red nails tangled in the curly black hair of a twenty-one-year-old construction worker named Eddie.

Shortly after this the police chief showed up at our house and told my mother that my behavior was giving the family a bad name. This reflected badly on my mother's brother who was a Grand Junction city councilman. My mother decided she could no longer handle me and sent me back to Bakersfield, California, to my father's house. In Bakersfield, I no longer had free reign and I resented it. I began to run away from home. After the second escape, Dad boarded me up in my bedroom for several months. The boards on the windows blocked out the sunlight. My siblings were enlisted as watchdogs; they were spanked if they did not report when I tried to escape. I felt hopeless, trapped like an animal. I spent my time plotting an escape plan. However, I never got the satisfaction of implementing it, because we moved to Oregon.

Once in Oregon I was no longer boarded up; but I continued my escape plans. I began stealing money from my dad and taking clothes to a locker in the bus terminal. As soon as I had accumulated enough, I boarded a bus for Sacramento, California, where my mother was then living with her new husband. I would not live with my father again. Before he died he cried and begged for my forgiveness and kept saying, "I don't know why I treated you so terribly, I just don't know why." Today I understand why I chose him for my father. He really forced me to fight for my life and my individuality.

Once living in Sacramento I alternately lived with my mother, who was a serious drunkard and addict, and lived on my own in an apartment. During this time I became pregnant twice. Since Mom still worked in a pharmacy, she brought home drugs to induce a spontaneous abortion.

At age fifteen I went back to Colorado to visit my sister and her husband. The husband welcomed me back by raping me. A couple days later I had consensual sex with him. Why not? The result was a baby girl. My mother and I agreed to keep the pregnancy a secret to protect my sister. However, my mother got drunk and told her anyway. My sister hated me for years after that.

Since I had already had two abortions, my mother insisted that I deliver this child and give it up for adoption to teach me a lesson. There I was, a sophomore in high school, and pregnant. I realized that I needed to save myself. I knew my violent and oppressive family would suffocate any life left in my spirit, so I quit school and got a job working at a cleaners. My boss helped set me up in an apartment. However, he had an ulterior motive. I returned the favor by paying him with sex.

By the time I was sixteen I was still on drugs, no longer in school, had had two abortions, and had given up a baby girl - a product of rape - for adoption. She was born May 9, 1961, in Sacramento, California. The most painful memory I have is giving away my daughter. She is thirty-nine now. I have begun looking for her.

After the baby was adopted, I was sent to live with my aunt and uncle in Grand Junction. My uncle was a politician. We have several politicians in my family. Strom Thurman is apparently a cousin of my grandfather, Curly O'Brien, a wild Irishman. My aunt and uncle were the first to teach me the basics in life, such as table manners and how to dress properly; they also put me through Beauty College. I was hell for my aunt to deal with because I was so rebellious; I was continually drinking and drugging, it was a difficult year at their home.

I turned out to be a great hairdresser. My boss gave me her beauty shop when she moved away. This began my career in business. After owning my own beauty shop in Grand Junction, I moved to Denver where I had another shop. I was financially supporting my mother, my stepfather, and our addictions.

At age eighteen I moved to Sacramento where I managed a beauty shop. I had a small motorcycle, wore a pink bikini everywhere I went, water-skied a lot, drank even more, and had many scabs on my knees from falling off my bike while riding under the influence. I then abandoned the business and moved to Hollywood, with dreams of diving into bigger and better things. I threw myself into the fast lane of drugs and alcohol. The lesser drugs were no longer enough. I wanted something stronger, something faster. I began snorting cocaine, while continuing to drink and take pills. I worked in a men's hair styling salon on Sunset Boulevard, right in the middle of the action. I was in a drug group and we would sit around with alcohol, pot and other drugs. When the group was preparing to take LSD, one person would be the designated driver in case we all decided to go meet God on the beach or wherever and wouldn't be able to find our way back home.

I met a man who turned me onto LSD. I loved smoking marijuana and dropping LSD into cups of tea or on sugar cubes (it was in liquid form in the early sixties). Often I would be on an acid trip, then go to work. I am sure people must have thought I was crazy. I took at least 200 acid trips. Acid opened many psychic doors for me. I'll never forget what the Other Side looks like, or seeing all the electrical wiring in my aura and in the auras of the people around me. By no means am I advocating taking drugs to become psychic. I now know that raising the kundalini in meditation does the same thing without the dangerous side-effects. Kundalini, which I discuss later in this book, is the innate firepower within the base of the spine that begins moving up the spine when we awaken spiritually; it opens all the chakras, including the third eye that gives us our magical psychic sight.

By using drugs to open my psychic gifts, I also did incredible damage to my physical body, which I am still healing. I created very destructive patterns of addiction that continue to haunt me. And I weakened and opened my aura to the influence of non-physical entities and other dark forces. Kundalini opens the third eye without damaging the body or weakening the aura. In fact, it is a powerful healing force that strengthens the body and aura and helps to clear blockages and negative patterns.

While in Los Angeles at age nineteen I met a man who taught me how to develop my psychic gifts. He taught me how to be a criminal and survive on the streets. He taught me how to feel and sense danger, and to always have eyes in the back of my head. He showed me how to have my radar active at all times. I have never stopped practicing and using the techniques he taught me. However, as I look back at my childhood I can see that I was always intuitive, psychic, and a healer. I was a caregiver and healer for sick and injured neighborhood animals. I was the minister of the small pet cemetery where I buried all the animals I could not heal.

By 1966 at the age of twenty-two I was selling cocaine and had a lot of money. I lived in a beautiful home in Mill Valley, California, overlooking the San Francisco Bay. One night while visiting L.A. for the weekend, I was drunk in a bar called Donkins Inn at Marina Del Rey. I was on my way back from the Ladies Room when I met this tall, handsome man who was to become my husband. His name was Dennis Richardson and he gave me his phone number. Later that night, at two in the morning, I called him. Dennis was a medical student and lived on the beach in Venice. I stayed with him for a month. Then we went to my home in Mill Valley to collect my belongings. We returned to Venice and were married on the beach. I was ecstatic! I wore a gown and veil, but no shoes! The women at the wedding were dressed up while the men wore Hawaiian shirts and cut-offs. I had a flower girl and ring-bearer. It seemed to be the perfect marriage.

The bad news is that Dennis was a heroin addict. He had shared an apartment during medical school with his professor who had cancer. Together they created their own pain-killer which was similar to heroin.

We moved to Malibu where we had a beautiful home on the beach. For five-and-a-half years Dennis and I lived together and continued our lifestyle of using and selling drugs. I was strung out on heroin and cocaine. I played "Little Miss Suzy Homemaker" in-between fixes. Soon my savings of thousands of dollars was gone. My body was beginning to show the stress from all the drugs; it was being poisoned, but did not want to die. Over the next two-and-a-half years, I was in and out of the hospital with different ailments - heart infection, pneumonia, spleen disorders, and a blood clot in my lung. Thank God I lived! At the time, my husband Dennis' body seemed to do fine with all the drugs. However, it all caught up with him eventually. He died in 1978 of an overdose of heroin and alcohol at age thirty-eight. His entire body was diseased with hepatitis, cancer, and more.

In 1968 at the age of twenty-three I had a beautiful baby boy, Kol. However, I was too sick to take care of him. I thank God for my family and friends who helped care for him, because I was near death. Each day I had to choose whether to spend my dollars for food or milk. When he was two-and-a-half years old, Social Services took Kol away from me and gave him to my sister to raise. Those were painful, painful times.

I can't even count the number of times I came out of a heroin overdose to find someone shooting milk or salt into my veins to bring me back. Or I would "come to" in a cold shower. Or I'd wake up in bed with Dennis giving me mouth-to-mouth resuscitation. One time I awoke on a cold, wet hospital lawn; that meant I had been dumped there by somebody who was unable to resuscitate me. That's what we did if someone died of an overdose or if we could not resuscitate him. Occasionally one or more of us would sit across the street waiting to see how soon the overdosed person would be discovered. But most of the time we simply dumped the body off and went on our merry way to the next "high."

One time I regained consciousness just as two junkies I knew were throwing me into a dumpster. I remember vividly seeing the dark tunnel with the brilliant white light at the end, where I was given the choice whether to stay or return to my body. I remember thinking about my son, Kol, and choosing to live. Now I know that I also chose to live so I can teach, not only my son, but myself and other people as well.

After Dennis and I parted in 1972, for the next twelve years I shot up (injected) methanphetamines (speed) and cocaine and drank a quart of vodka a day. In 1972-73 I struggled to get off heroin. During that time, I hitchhiked back and forth across the western United States several times. I would leave Los Angeles to escape the temptations there and head for Colorado. But each time I'd get drunk, stick out my thumb, and wind up back in L.A. again. I'd arrive sick and craving heroin. I knew that I would never meet a heroin connection in Denver or Boulder. L.A. was the place for such connections.

I finally succeeded in getting off heroin, and in 1973, when Kol was six, I drove to Boulder, Colorado, where he was living with my sister. I whisked him away. I took him to Chicago, Florida, then back to Denver. I was still very addicted to speed and cocaine. But by this time I didn't have many useable veins left in my feet, ankles, legs, arms, or hands. (By the time I finally quit in 1982, I was using my jugular vein. And now, after eighteen years of being clean and sober, I am beginning to get some surface veins back.)

In addition to the continuing toll on my physical body, I was also mentally unstable. In fact, I was nuts, off the wall, totally crazy. I have many bizarre tales from those years. I have spoken about them in Narcotics Anonymous meetings. Perhaps one day I will be able to write about them.

As I continued the life of addiction, my angry, violent tendencies grew. I began carrying a gun everywhere I went. I ran with a dangerous crowd. I attempted suicide many times, and my relatives placed bets on how long I would last. They were all wrong.

By the age of twenty-eight I was on probation for two years for counterfeiting. I was well enough to attend college. Dad had always told me I was stupid and would never amount to anything. Much to my surprise, I loved school! After all those years of believing I was stupid, I was shocked to discover that, not only was I not stupid, I was getting A's. My major was psychology and my minor was sociology. However, before I could graduate, I began drinking and using drugs again. I lived with another guy. Today he too is clean and sober, one of the few who made it. I think the odds are one in a thousand for someone to make it out of the street life.

There are a few tales I will share from those years. I met a man connected with the Mafia, or the "Big Boys." I'll call him Donald. He and I lived together. He bought five pounds of cocaine every two weeks. We shot up most of it and sold the rest. Even this did not always last and we'd have to go searching for more. Finally the "Big Boys" came to him and offered him a paid vacation to the Bahamas. They also mentioned, casually, that if he didn't stop shooting up their profits, they would shoot him. They didn't mind if he snorted (sniffed) it, but it was not okay to shoot up. They knew that an addict who shot drugs was a very dangerous and risky person to have working for them. For weeks he raged around the house and kept saying he wanted to die. Unfortunately, I was there when he got his wish.

Donald's death was a terrible thing to watch. He was shot through the heart while standing on a chair singing "Old Rugged Cross." I saw him fall. His eyes rolled up into his head, his pants fell down, blood gushed out like a pump, and he toppled forward onto the carpet and into his own blood. I didn't call for help until all evidence of drugs was out of sight. I scurried around the house hiding everything, then began screaming hysterically. When the paramedics arrived I was still in shock. I asked, "Is he still breathing? Is he alive?" A lovely black woman answered me, "No, honey, he won't be takin' any more breaths."

In another incident - a "war story" as we call them in Narcotics Anonymous and Alcoholics Anonymous - while I was conducting a drug deal, I was robbed inside an apartment building by three men. One of the men punched me in the face and I fell backwards, stunned, onto the floor. He came down on top of me with his fist above his head, gripping a knife. The blade came down on me before I could react, and he sliced my eyelid in half. I screamed hysterically. Then as I discovered I could see daylight through my eyelid, rage bubbled up from the pit of my stomach. I screamed, "You cut my eyelid, you son-of-a-bitch!" Fearlessly, I grabbed the knife with my right hand, cutting my thumb down to the bone. I threw the knife into my left hand, cutting that hand too, and punched him in the face as hard as my inner fire would let me. His body tumbled off me from the impact. I crawled out to the street, screaming hysterically, but no one would help me. There was blood everywhere. People stared at me, but quickly walked past. Finally, a motorcycle police officer came to my aid.

An incredible doctor, John A. Grossman, who is still practicing medicine in Denver (plastic surgery now), mended my thumb by splitting the tendon from my forefinger, lining half of the tendon in my thumb, drilling a hole through my thumb nail, and wiring the tendon to the bone. I was kept in the hospital in shock for a week. I was too traumatized to be released any sooner. After I got out of the hospital, I put a pistol in my sling and set out to find the men who did this. I did get even. They went back to prison.

Stories such as these abound in my past. Many of them are about being possessed by demons and being caught in the dark side of life for many years. I went through many years of sick relationships and many broken bones - back, ribs, wrist, foot, ankle, and nose. These injuries sent me back and forth to the hospital. I ruptured a disk in my spine and was in traction for a week. I proceeded to go out, get drunk, and fall down on the dance floor and rupture the same disc again. Then I broke my sacrum jumping off a porch. I thought my boyfriend would catch me; instead, we both went tumbling. I broke my wrist, wore a cast for six weeks, fell down drunk and broke it again. I also have had several whiplash injuries from rolling trucks and other accidents. Life was so very painful. But I never took it seriously, because I assumed I would not live long. Most addicts don't.

My life was violent. As I mentioned, I had been carrying a gun for years. I never shot anyone, but I fought a lot. I've done barroom brawling; I've been beaten and I've beaten others, mostly men. I became more and more dangerous as time went on. I have pictures of myself from those years and I don't even resemble that hard, dangerous woman.

They say you have to hit rock bottom before you can quit addictive behavior. But, damn, I seemed to be at rock bottom for so very, very long. It wasn't until I stabbed my boyfriend that it was time for divine intervention. In May 1982 I was living with yet another drunk I had taken home with me from detox. He was full of rage and beat me up twice. I always chose men who beat me, just like Dad.

I could spot a loser and abuser in a room of 500 people and magnetically draw him to me. The subconscious pattern sent a silent message: "Hey, you remind me of my dangerous, sick father. Will you come home and beat me up like he did? Oh, come on, I'll even support you and buy all the alcohol. What else are daughters for?"

So, Gerald fit the parameters of this sick pattern. He had hit black-out stage in his alcoholism. When he drank his darkness came through him. He'd act out violently, then not remember any of it the next day. In those years I was known as Crazy Patti. One evening my friend, Crazy Mary, was visiting me. We got those nicknames on the street because no one ever knew what we would do next, not even us. We were pretty dangerous.

I was frying steaks on the stove and cutting cucumbers. Gerald came into the kitchen, grabbed the frying pan, and threw it on the floor. Hot grease splattered everywhere. I glared at him. As our eyes met, something snapped inside of me. I literally saw red as the rage consumed me. I still had the butcher knife in my hand from slicing the cucumbers. I don't know where I went in that instant, or who I became, or who or what took over, but when I finally came back to reality, he was lying on the floor with blood seeping through his clothes. This time it was his blood, not mine!

I glanced at Mary, grabbed the keys to the pickup truck, and calmly said, "Let's go shoot some pool." It wasn't until an hour later that I realized my own foot had been cut in my frenzy of rage. The guy who was shooting pool with me asked, "What's all that blood from?"

I replied, "Oh, I must have cut myself, too." His eyes grew to the size of pancakes. He laid the pool stick down on the table and backed away from me.

The next day I returned to the house and found Gerald in bed. There was blood everywhere. His brother had taken him to the hospital. I had stabbed him multiple times. I realized I was in serious trouble with drugs and alcohol. I would eventually kill someone if I didn't seek help, and seek it soon. I stormed into an Alcoholic's Anonymous meeting yelling and crying, "Somebody, please help me!"

They drove me to detox. I heard God say, "This is it, Patti. It's over!" On June 19, 1982, at the age of thirty-seven, I quit drinking and using drugs. Another exciting thing that happened was somebody told me a guy had spoken at an Alcoholic's Anonymous meeting and told his group he had quit drinking after this crazy drunk woman stabbed him several times. Gerald and I both quit alcohol and became aligned with spirit, God, the higher self or whatever you chose to call your higher power. I hope he is still sober.

I had been living in a small apartment with my mom, step-dad, and my son at the time I quit the dark, hellish life. My step-dad had quit alcohol nine months earlier at the age of sixty-five. He almost died from seizures as he came off the alcohol. My mom quit one year later, but while I was living there she was still drinking. As I looked at the situation around me, I said, "That's it. I have to find a few years of joy." I knew I could not stay sober in that apartment with my mother still drinking. I decided I had to live alone so I could heal. I moved to a house further down the street to stay near my son, Kol, now age fourteen.

People often ask, "How did you do it?" I used to say, "By the grace of God," and this is true. However, it's difficult to answer because so many addicts and alcoholics don't recover. I feel there was divine intervention, that a miracle happened, and that I had finished paying off old karma. Now, I tell people that one day I was drinking and drugging, and the next day it was over. I was reborn.

My spirit has always had strength and tenacity, and I was given a second chance. I call this "my second life in this life."

During my first year without drugs or alcohol I was a basket case. I was functional enough to work as a bartender. Amazing, isn't it? I went back to pouring drinks. But I also found the strength to join Narcotics Anonymous and Alcoholics Anonymous. I am still an active member.

One of the reasons I "made it" was because God gave me an incredible gift: I was given a wonderful, wacko, weird man who became my sponsor and my teacher in the twelve-step program. Many argued then that I would do better with a woman sponsor. But Bob W. was perfect for me. He helped me change my whole life and begin my spiritual life. There are no mistakes. I knew Bob would be perfect as my teacher. He came to my apartment every night to pick me up. He would say, "Come on, Heroin Patti (my nickname in the program), let's go to a meeting." When I resisted, he would stand there, often with other friends, until I agreed to go to the meetings. One of the great aspects of these twelve-step programs is the support that each member gives to the others. Anytime I was depressed or scared, I was told to call Bob or other members and find someone to help me. This always worked. And I, in turn, was available to them. I was "the ride" to the meetings for those who didn't have a car.

I moved into a house with seven other recovering addicts. I did not miss a daily meeting for seven months. Every day I went in and made the coffee. I was group representative for several meetings and started meetings at new locations. Still today there is a core group of us who remember the good-old days and the sense of community when we all looked out for each other.

Bob took me through the "twelve steps" the first

time. Some of these include turning our lives over to God, writing a list of all the people we are angry with and discovering our part in the drama, confessing all of this by reading it to someone, apologizing to all of the people on the list, and being willing to make all things right and be forgiven by God. In addition, we are to pray and meditate every day and help others do the same.

The steps are phenomenal. I was able to be around alcohol without the desire to drink. I learned how to simply remove myself from the presence of drugs. I did apologize to every person I had ever harmed in my life. Most of them responded with tears and forgiveness. Some I could not locate, so Bob had me read my amends to him and to God.

As I mentioned, that first year was very difficult. I had abscesses all over my body from injecting drugs. I was terribly scarred and broken - physically, mentally, emotionally, and spiritually. I spent hours sitting in a chair or in bed crying, shivering, and shaking. My nervous system was shot. I was terrified to even talk to other people. I had panic attacks. If I went to a party, I'd sit there praying that no one would ask me to dance. My sponsor advised me to have no sexual relationships for at least a year. With a few exceptions, it turned out to be seven years. For this I am grateful, because I was able to break the pattern of abusive and dysfunctional sexual relationships.

At Bob's advice I began service work and sponsored many other people myself. He encouraged me to read spiritual literature and guided me to many esoteric and mystical books such as the Don Juan books by Carlos Castaneda, *Grist for the Mill* and *Be Here Now* by Ram Dass, and *Sermon on the Mount* from the Bible.

The process I have gone through - and indeed, am still going through - on my path to enlightenment has been both painful and exciting because, when I finally woke up and came out of the fog of a lifetime of alcohol and drugs, I had a lot of repair work to do. My emotions were distorted and my physical body was seriously malfunctioning, especially my nervous and digestive systems. I had broken many bones, including my back. The memories of childhood-abuse were stored in my tissues. For many years when the cellular memories were re-stimulated I shook and shivered as I experienced flashbacks of past events. I had an old belief system deeply ingrained into my nervous system and DNA from this and past lives that kept me repeating the same destructive patterns over and over again. I still occasionally have flashbacks, but I no longer react physically.

In 1984 after two years of abstinence from substances, except cigarettes (which I did quit in 1989), I found kundalini. A man came to Denver and distributed posters all over the city. I was drawn to this man who extolled liberation and freedom from the bondage's of the self (lower ego). After years of experiencing the highest of highs on drugs, I wondered if what he was saying could be true. Could I achieve bliss by meditation and the kundalini experience?

I was still a novice at all the spiritual stuff. Bob, my Narcotic's Anonymous sponsor, had instructed me to meditate twice a day. The kundalini teacher made five or six appearances in Denver. The first time I saw him there were 400 people in the room. He said he would give us all shakti (feminine kundalini energy) by looking into our eyes. We meditated with him. When he looked into my eyes I began to see psychically wild colors and auras just like when I had dropped a lot of LSD. It was the same experience. Naturally, I went to see him every time I could. He called groups together for about a week and a half. My psychic portals were opened again and I was thrilled to know I could access higher states from this kundalini energy.

He explained that there is an energy center residing at

the base of the spine, like a serpent coiled up and waiting to be awakened. As the serpent rises, the energy moves up the spine. You can feel it move. It is either hot or cool as it moves up the spine and through all of the chakras. It purifies all organs, glands, bones, and the skin. Then it moves out through the aura. All of this is explained in detail in this book.

After meditating with this teacher I became hooked on kundalini. It was exciting to sit around every day and meditate. I sat in a dark room gazing at a candle, chanting, doing breath work, and spinning my chakras for hours every day for a couple of weeks. I experienced ecstasy. I did not want to leave that room. My son wondered what the heck had happened to his mother. My friends in Narcotics Anonymous reacted with disbelief when I told them I had found a substitute for cocaine that was even more powerful. They thought I had flipped my lid. Why would anyone want to get high on anything after being clean from drugs? And I'm sure that most people cannot comprehend the blissful intoxication that comes from kundalini energy unless they have experienced it.

One day I had a spontaneous kundalini rising that was the most powerful, blissful thing I had ever experienced. I heard what sounded like a train blasting up my back and into my head, and in my mind's eye I saw amazing fire. I felt a volcano of energy shoot out the top of my head, creating a beautiful fountain that fell down around my body. All at once I became nothing and everything. I knew I was having a full body experience of the light of God. It was better than any drug I had ever taken. It also terrified me. I panicked. The fear of total loss of control rushed over me.

Of course, the addict inside of me loved this tremendous power. And, of course, compelled by the addictive part of me, I overdid the meditation and breathing exercises. I was trying to force the kundalini. All of the warnings about abusing kundalini power and prematurely forcing it are true. I ended up with my right eye swollen shut and I kept walking into walls and lifting off the floor (levitating). But I still loved it.

Once I recognized this new version of my old destructive patterns of addiction, I had to completely stop the intense discipline, take a step back, and allow the kundalini to clear me in its own time.

In 1984 I became involved with a group of channelers in an organization called the Tibetan Foundation. I joined because I had started having an odd experience every night. I would awaken at four to four-thirty a.m. and find myself talking out loud and standing in weird positions (e.g., standing on one foot with my arms in certain positions). I now know these were mudras, yoga positions. Words were coming out of my mouth, but I was not conscious enough to understand what they were. It seemed mighty unusual to me! I mentioned these experiences to a friend, Randall, who had been involved in the metaphysical world for many years. He said it sounded like I was channeling. He suggested that I leave a pen and paper beside my bed, and program my mind to write down what was being channeled through me. This sort of worked. When I awoke, I would be writing all over my nightgown in addition to the paper. And I could not make out any of the words. I went back to Randall and he suggested the Tibetan Foundation.

They met every Tuesday night and different people channeled the ascended masters such as Jesus, St. Germaine, Djwhal Kuhl, and Vywamus. I went to a meeting with Randall and was very excited. It was a new beginning for me. At the time I was working as a waitress and bartender and was still wondering what I was going to do professionally with the rest of my life. The Tibetan Foundation offered different courses and had a membership base of 800 to 1,000 people. Almost all of the members were psychotherapists, psychologists, healers, and teachers. With my college course work in psychology and sociology, this was right up my alley; plus, there were "weirdos" in the group teaching the far-out metaphysical information. I was in psychological and airy-fairy heaven. The best of both worlds.

Up to this time I had been deeply involved in service work in the twelve-step programs. My sponsor had insisted, and correctly so, that in order to recover, I had to get out of myself and help others. As I became more and more involved in metaphysics, I shifted my service work focus to the Tibetan Foundation.

In my new life, in my new organization, I took every class I could. I learned hundreds of different techniques to clear the subconscious mind of the negative beliefs and programming that stood in the way of creating and manifesting through love and unlimitedness. Many of these are presented in this book. I became deeply involved in healing and conscious channeling. Conscious channeling means allowing the masters and angels to speak through us while we remain consciously present and aware of what we are saying.

At this time in 1984 I also personally addressed the problem of nonpositive entities. In order to channel positive, light beings, I had to first clean out the dark beings. Throughout the years of drinking and using drugs, I had weakened my aura and accumulated many nonphysical beings who were not of the highest good. I spent six months undergoing an intense process in order to be cleared of these entities. They had found a house (my body) that they did not want to vacate. I went through many different exorcisms and processes, some of which frightened me, some of which also frightened others. Those were interesting times, to say the least. I later learned there were a lot of people who awakened during 1984 and I thank God I was one of them.

It was so very exciting to awaken to this new world of truths and to have such a wonderful opportunity to learn so many valuable things. When I look back on the opportunities that were laid out before me at that time, it becomes clear that God has a grand plan for the universe and that each one of us has his/her own part in this great play. As Shakespeare wrote, all of us are actors upon the stage.

Another aspect I delved into during those years was religion. I began visiting many different churches and groups. I went to revival meetings, gospel singing, tent meetings, Jewish synagogues, and churches of the Presbyterian, Methodist, fundamentalist, Buddhist, and Lutheran faiths. You name it, I went there. I needed to experience every belief and philosophy available. Soon I was reading as many books as possible. I became very active in the Tibetan Foundation and taught the workshops and classes that I had once taken on channeling and clearing. I spent two years doing tapes for people to use at home in the evenings. People would send a few dollars with a theme area they wanted to clear, such as unworthiness, fear, anger, laziness, etc. I would channel a tape giving the person a past life experience that related to the issue and also channel exercises and methods for the person to use to clear the issue.

Being the extremist I was, I paid attention to what I was channeling for others and did all of the clearing exercises myself! I became obsessed with clearing, to say the least. Unfortunately I believed that because I had experienced such an awful life, because I had hurt so many people, I must be so much further "behind" all the others who were also clearing their issues. I thought I needed to clear deeper and more intensely than anyone else. I also believed I needed to be punished severely and do penance for my misdeeds. I was my own harshest judge. And in my self-judgment and obsession, I took the same intensity and addictive behavior that had powered my life of darkness and focused it on my healing. I turned healing into an addiction! I became a workaholic as a healer of others and myself. I worked many hours each day and seven days a week. I now see the logic and wisdom in moderation and I no longer treat myself like that; but I don't know that I really could have changed much because of the addictive patterns that were still engrained in me. I must assume this was the way I needed to undertake my transformation.

During my life of drugs and alcohol I developed many survival skills that today have become my intuitive gifts. To protect myself, I became adept at using my "radar" to scan everyone and everything around me, looking for drug money, danger, cops, etc. At some point I figured out that I did not process information like most people. At the time I thought I was flawed. I often felt like I had been dropped off on the wrong planet. But through my healing journey, I began to see these abilities as intuitive gifts that could be used to serve the light and help people, instead of being used to guide and protect me during a life of darkness.

In 1985 I began my practice as an intuitive counselor. During my first year I made a great deal of money. This money was more important than the cocaine money because I worked hard for it, and it was legal. Most of that money was spent in search of that very God who had handed me the gift of rebirth.

The Tibetan Foundation was centered in Sedona, Arizona. I made several trips there two or three times a year, meeting with hundreds of other people for seminars and convocations. I was in Sedona in August 1987 for the Harmonic Convergence which, according to information received through channeling, was a major initiation for planet Earth during which she merged with her soul. One of the reasons why these times are so facilitating for healing and enlightenment is because the growth is happening on so many levels. The entire planet is going through this ascension process with us. We are all ascending into a lighter, higher vibration. We are all becoming light, so we are all becoming less dense. (I discuss initiations, soul merge, and ascension later in this book.)

Eventually the Tibetan Foundation came to a stop. Janet McClure, the founder, was traveling abroad most of the time and the politics became complicated in the Denver group. At the time I was on the Board of Directors. Those of us who had been channeling and devoting our time and energy to the organization for years all hit a place of burnout. People were moving on. Frankly, I think these pioneer channels had finished their mission. As I look back, it appears as though there were several waves of teachers and organizations in the 1980s that came forth to bring us the message of ascension. There were mystery schools, eastern gurus, extraterrestrial/UFO groups, and shamans. Great books were written during that decade and I was fortunate to be a part of the movement. Many of us who were channels then are writing books now. A lot of the material channeled through Janet McClure, the founder of the Tibetan Foundation, recently has been published in Prelude to Ascension: Tools for Transformation.

After the Tibetan Foundation ended, some of the members began taking journeys to sacred places such as India, Egypt, and Peru. In 1988 I visited India for the first time. I traveled with twenty-four other former Foundation members from all over the world. In Northern India, we did the tourist thing and visited palaces and temples, such as the Taj Majal. The palaces were incredible! I saw lapis work with inlaid gems; marble, onyx and jade floors; gold-plated ceilings; engraved silver doors. Uniformed guards kept the palaces safe as we strolled through in the warm November heat.

In Southern India we began our spiritual pilgrimage. We saw cities, mosques (tombs), and many wonderful people and places. In Putaparti we stayed for three days with at least 20,000 other people to see a guru named Sai Baba and celebrate his birthday. The only place for us to stay was in the dormitories which were huge buildings with bathrooms, showers, and lots of floor space. We rented cots and were each assigned a six-by-four-foot rectangle on the floor. Our day began at four a.m. with bajans (singing prayers) and chants. Then thousands of people gathered for the darshan, the "meeting in the presence of a saint." It was ecstatic! The energy was very intense. So intense, in fact, that by the time I reached the London Airport on the way home, I had major symptoms of hepatitis. Apparently, Sai Baba's kundalini energy at the darshan was so high that it activated, brought up, and released into my system the chronic hepatitis that had been lying dormant in my liver for twenty years. Time to clear it!

I was sick in bed for six months. It proved to be one of the most important growth experiences for me. I was forced to allow my roommate, who was an apprentice to me in my counseling work, to cook and care for me. For someone with as big an ego as I had, this was a very humbling time in my life. Oh, yes, the ego is still with me. It takes a long time to grow through it. Haven't gotten there yet.

While I was down in bed I was terrified that I would not be able to sustain myself financially. And miracles happened. My friend, Bill Livermore, hired me to do distant healing on people, some personal and some business. This helped greatly with the money issue. Then God sent me another angel. Her name was Dorothy Rome. She called and asked if the rumors were true that I was bedridden. Then she asked if she could stop by for a couple of minutes. I said "yes" to both questions. This incredible eighty-year-old angel came in the door with bag after bag of groceries, spiritual books for me to read, and a beautiful plant. She made me a bowl of soup, lit a candle for me, sprinkled glitter all over my body, and on her way out the door she left a $500 check on the desk. Truly these people were messengers of light and love. I know that they were sent to me by God.

After a year of healing I was again starved for spiritual knowledge and wisdom. I wandered from spiritual master to teacher to organization. Eventually, in 1989, I found a spiritual kundalini yoga organization of which I am still a member today. This organization teaches high level values and a practical way to live. They do not advertise, but they are so powerful, magnetic, and loving that there are millions of members, and I am proud to be one of them. I found a spiritual master, or maybe she found me. I feel so blessed for this protection, love, and grace. I am now physically in her presence at least once or twice a year.

For the past fifteen years I have helped counsel and heal thousands of people. I do individual therapy sessions and teach classes in meditation, intuitive development, and healing. I also teach kundalini workshops where people can find their inner strength, power, self-love, abundance, and can clear away the past to find their personal freedom.

Today I host and produce a TV talk show in Denver called Patrisha: Mystical Insights. It is a weekly show I took over from another host in 1993. I teach spiritual exercises, techniques, and values each week, and I interview different guests on various topics within the healing and metaphysical community. I love doing the show because it exposes me to so much fascinating information. I usually know something about the topic, but I am thrilled to learn more details along with the studio and viewing audience. I give intuitive readings to the audience the second half of the show.

For seven years I was single and very independent, but desperately wanted love and a mate; however I was too afraid to allow someone into my life. When I did date, I placed so many restrictions and judgments on the relationships and the men, that our time together was doomed to failure. This was one area of life that I did not feel would ever be pleasing or fulfilling. How could it? I had to remain in control; the fear of losing control kept me locked in the fear and, of course, kept me single.

Then, in the fall of 1993 I was given a gift. This precious gift was the most wonderful mate! Paul is spiritual, funny, and has a loving heart. He has helped me open my heart. I now know that I could not have opened my heart as quickly without a loving, physical mate to help me. My godself had drawn him in because I finally understand I am worthy and loveable. It took me years of healing and clearing to get to that point.

Paul is also open to learning. He can handle the kundalini energy coming from my body. He is open to Eastern Indian scriptures. He loves God, meditation, and chanting. We made an agreement in the beginning that I would teach him spiritual things and he would teach me healthy eating and physical fitness because he knows so much about these. We have never felt more or less than each other because we know that our strengths are in different areas. Now we have been together for more than six years. We always encourage each other. For instance, we remind each other to feed the body if it is weak or we are irritable. We also remind each other to chant, meditate, and pray if we feel disconnected from our spiritual path, each other, or our work.

After being single for seventeen years (except for

very short relationships) while working on my spiritual path, I was so far removed from what constitutes a healthy relationship that I assumed Paul would teach me. He had almost never been single. But, to our surprise, neither of us knew experientially about healthy relationships. It has been a wonderful growing experience for us (most of the time). We base our love relationship on our spiritual path together. And our relationship with God is number one. If we find ourselves off course, we lovingly nudge each other back to God.

When I met Paul he was living in Canada. He continued to live there for two-and-a-half years. We saw each other every two or three months, talked on the phone nearly every night (oh, the phone bills!), and traveled together to beautiful and romantic places as well as to spiritual retreats, until he was able to move to Denver to live with me. He was here three-and-a-half years, then moved to Los Angeles for a year to pursue his acting career (more phone bills!). Now we are together again in Denver. We belong to the same spiritual organization and practice our disciplines. Although we experienced long distance love for long periods, and it was painful for us, "it was okay" because our love is strong and we have been able to maintain our identities and individuality. We both continue to work on our spiritual enlightenment and I find that this love is healthy and profound. Actually, I don't know if I would have been able to stay in the relationship if we were together all these years because I needed the space to grow and trust him. I had such serious issues with men due to my childhood. I could have chased him away.

In November 1993 at the same time I met Paul and was given the television program, I also reconciled my relationship with my son, Kol. He had been resentful toward me for years. Finally, when his daughter was born, he wanted to be close to me again. I had yearned for a relationship with Kol for so long and had experienced such guilt from the abuse he had suffered from me as a drug-addicted and alcoholic mother. I had felt a tremendous loss, always being estranged from him. Being close to him now is a major marker of joy in my life. Interesting how things all come together. That year, something must have clicked in astrologically and/or emotionally and spiritually on all levels at once. I thank my spirit for bringing these wonderful gifts to me.

I have been devoted to my spiritual path for what seems an eternity, and surely it is. Each year there seems to be just a little more knowing of who I am as a light being, and a little more ego is dissolved and I am lifted up into higher consciousness. There is more love for myself and for others. When I look back at my life and all of the people I interacted with, the script becomes obvious for each person: all the variables, all the choices, at all the crossroads. With our own free will, we choose one path or another. All lead to the top of the mountain. All paths are different, just like all people are different. Our paths are made up out of our uniqueness in our essence and DNA, as well as all past experience in this life and lives before. I chose to burn off my karma by doing drugs, alcohol, and living a life of hell until the karma was finally finished. Then, like a child, I was led by the hand from one organization to another in order to clear out the old and bring in the new powerful behaviors. The power that I harnessed is not the lower self or ego power. It is the power of love, unconditional love, which is the ultimate goal.

My physical body continues to be a successful, ongoing healing process. I have almost finished repairing the damage from the years of abuse. In the last two years I have changed my diet, I'm on herbal programs, and I do a physical fitness program with a personal trainer. I have quit drinking coffee and diet soda (most of the time!) My intake of dairy and sugar is minimal. When I started this healing process I felt old, used up, pathetic, and fat. I had been a chronic dieter for years, gaining and losing the same ten pounds over and over. Today I am at a weight I am comfortable with.

The script of my recovery could not have been better written. It was an incredible growing process of becoming part of the God Force. When I say, "God Force," I mean the beautiful force of which we are all a part. As Deepak Chopra tells us, we are all part of one another; our higher selves and our atomic particles are all one. We merge into each other's auras and feel, hear, think, and experience other people's lives.

As I sit here writing this book, my aura is bigger than I know and actually spreads out over the city block, the city, the state, the planet, and the universe. We are all very massive beings and stretch from the heavens through the earth and out again in all directions. All at once, and all at the same time. We are huge. Therefore, we know all things and each lifetime is an opportunity to remember who we really are, and to be that once again, to remember "I am that I am," which means I am God. If we already know we are God, then our purpose in life becomes clearer, because our purpose is to serve God and humankind. But to accomplish this, we must become clear mentally and emotionally by removing the nonpositive beliefs and feelings about ourselves and replacing them with positive thoughts of truth, light, and love. We need to allow our higher self to merge with our lower self so we can remember and honor who we are which is the All Perfect Self.

I love any opportunity to teach people that a painful, abusive childhood in darkness does not mean that the light of God is far out of reach. The cycle of violence can be stopped with any of us at any time. Healing begins the second we realize this. My life is truly an example of this. I love life! I choose to find the gift in all things today, even if I have to dig down deep to find it. Sometimes it takes a while. Sometimes I feel awful for long periods. But I always know there is a pot of gold at the end of the rainbow and, if not, I'll create one. My self and my reality are what I create with my thoughts, emotions, and intent.

In my own healing process and in my counseling work, I have learned hundreds of techniques for healing the mind, body, spirit, and emotions. This book presents many of these. It also presents what I have learned about ascension and the enlightenment process. I am so glad I was able to awaken in this lifetime, so I can be here to participate and serve as the planet and its people undergo this grand ascension process. What a celebration!

Patrisha Richardson
Denver, Colorado
March, 2000

INTRODUCTION

Introduction

*t*his book is a guide for people like you and me who are on our spiritual paths. Hopefully, my perceptions about my own path of enlightenment fit closely enough to your own that you will feel comfortable reading this book.

I think it is fair to say that I have been on a spiritual path of enlightenment for many lifetimes. And so have you. For me, this particular lifetime has seemed like many lifetimes in one; I don't know how many, but there've been a lot! This life that I chose certainly has not been boring, I must say, not even for a moment. If you read "Patrisha's Story" (my bio), you already know I chose some very interesting parents, that I spent twenty-five years addicted to drugs and alcohol while living a life of violence and crime on the streets, and that I awoke to spirit in my late thirties and became a healer. I can see now, in retrospect, that I chose those very difficult years for a fast path to awareness, ultimately coming to understanding that I was not a victim of circumstances.

In the following chapters, I share many of the techniques and methods I have used on myself and with clients to become clearer each day and each year. Some of them I learned in the numerous classes and workshops I attended through the years, some of them were shown to me by my guidance, some are composites of pieces from various sources. I am always open to using my creativity to modify these techniques, so most have changed and continue to change through the years.

That is part of the magic. The more we clear away the old, nonpositive beliefs about ourselves, the more pure and creative we become. At our core, we hold all possibilities, ideas, formulas, potentials, love, artistic abilities, and strengths. The more layers we peel off the "onion" of our limiting beliefs, the closer we get to our core Self.

This book covers a wide range of material. The first chapter discusses intuitive gifts and how we use them to contact our spiritual guidance in order to gather information about ourselves and other people. The second chapter introduces the chakras and bodies that compose our energy fields. This material lays the groundwork for the third chapter about hands-on healing. Many aspect and techniques of hands-on healing are covered, including implants, grounding, and protection. Step-by-step instructions are given for performing a hands-on healing. I also discuss techniques for performing an "absentee" healing on someone who is not physically present.

Chapters four, five, and six discuss in detail many of the techniques and exercises that I use for emotional and mental body clearing and healing. These cover a wide range of topics, such as inner-child work, past-life regression, soul retrieval, releasing attachments and entities, and career transitioning. Chapter seven presents a brief look at extraterrestrials. The final two chapters cover the advanced subjects of kundalini and ascension. The kundalini information discusses this powerful spiritual energy and gives exercises for activating it. The chapter on ascension covers one of the most exciting aspects of my healing work: facilitating initiation ceremonies. The various levels of initiation are described as I experience them in myself and others. I also include guidelines for facilitating the ceremonies.

I hope from the bottom of my heart that you will benefit from what I give you in this book. Life can be experienced from a sense of peace. Life is to be enjoyed. A sense of humor is critical! Part of the goal of healing is to learn to laugh at ourselves from a witness position and to see how funny we are in all of our seriousness. We love to take everything too seriously because it complicates everything, which forces us into our mind to figure out our problems instead of feeling the experiences and instead of enjoying life. So, let's have fun and clear ourselves into a state of bliss!

ONE

Accessing Information and Developing Your Intuitive Gifts

INTUITIVE GIFTS

*W*e use our intuitive gifts to access information that lies beyond the physical senses. We can receive this information directly from other people by hearing their thoughts, feeling their emotions, and/or seeing their energy fields. We can also use our intuitive gifts to access information from our higher self and nonphysical beings such as our spiritual guides.

The four common intuitive gifts are seeing (clairvoyance), hearing (clairaudience), feeling (clairsentience), and knowing or prophesy (presentience, or precognition). These are the gifts created by the chakras of the body; therefore, these gifts are of an earthly nature. As we undergo the enlightenment process, these gifts develop into higher intuition. That is the true gift.

Seeing, or clairvoyance, comes from the third eye chakra. If you have ever seen a light or a glow around a person, you were seeing the aura. After further development of this gift, you will begin to see colors. You can practice using this gift by turning down the lights and gazing at yourself in a mirror for about ten minutes. Or you can gaze at another person; but, instead of focusing directly on the person, gaze about two feet in front of him or her.

Hearing, clairaudience, comes from the throat chakra and around the back of the head. For instance, if you are listening to an angel, master, or guide, you may be looking off to one side for instruction or information. Always remember, the information is only as clear or high in spiritual nature as the person who is receiving the message. Be cautious to whom you give away your power by taking someone's advice. You may very well be more intuitive than your local psychic. Check out your own inner spiritual information first. Then if the psychic gives you the same information, you have been validated and can start trusting yourself more.

It is very important to protect yourself before accessing guidance. Always ask Christ or a master to surround you with "white light" and protect you from lower astral beings (dark spirits from the other side). (See "Protection Techniques" in chapter three for additional suggestions.) Always pay attention to the level of the message. If there is swearing, or earth-based level information, you may have connected to the wrong spiritual phone number. Go higher!

The intuitive gift of feeling comes from the third chakra, the feeling center in the front of the body. An example is the knot you get in your stomach when you are frightened. That's a warning that something's wrong. This chakra contracts to protect you by not taking in something harmful. Always trust your feelings! Some people always have a knot in their stomach because they are ultra sensitive. The solar plexus chakra can be damaged if this response pattern isn't healed. Some people have an oversized third chakra that may be longer and bigger because they routinely use it to scan for the sake of protection. They use this chakra like the whiskers on a cat or the antenna on an insect.

Something that always gets my attention is a person who gets right up in my face and pushes against the chakras in my emotional body (we have chakras in all of our "subtle" bodies, which are discussed in chapter two). When they do this, I can't feel their aura and I can't use my radar to feel if I am safe or not. I feel like I'm being taken advantage of. I immediately back up in order to feel, look, and intuit what this person is all about. I also am leery of those instant huggers who grab you the minute you walk in the door. They are usually after something, even if it is only your energy. Yes, your energy. People can be psychic vampires who suck you dry in seconds by pressing up against your chakras. It is like they're at the pump at the energy service station and you are the source. You'll know you have been "attacked": when you have just enough energy left to go find a place to sit for a while to recharge your own battery! So take care of your feeling center. You can smooth the front of your aura by making upward sweeping movements about three inches out from your body with the flat of your hand.

Knowing is the prophesy gift. You are able to predict what the future holds. This gift is accessed from the higher chakras around the head. It is the rarest of gifts, and one of the truest. Edgar Cayce was a modern-day prophet. Nostradamus was an earlier prophet. Both of these men had the ability to foresee the future, and both were surprisingly correct. A prophet knows things. If you hear a person say often, "I know," he or she just very well may.

Once you determine your gift order, it becomes easier to understand how you are perceiving and communicating. For instance, if you are a seer and feeler, take note which you do first. Here is a test for you. Walk over to a plant in your home, close your eyes and gently touch a leaf. Do you feel that the leaf is bigger than you have seen it, or does it feel the same size? If the leaf feels bigger, you are probably a seer first. In other words, you have seen the leaf at one size and it is a surprise to you that it feels larger.

You can also pay attention to the order in which you receive messages by writing down how you received the information. For example, you walk into a room and you are introduced to a man. Your first impression is the most important. Consciously break down your response to him. At the first opportunity, write your impressions. Did you feel his aura? Did you see something that helped you decide who this person is? Did you hear something in his voice that was an indicator of his character? Or did you just know who this person is? By writing these experiences down you can learn a lot about your gifts. It becomes very exciting when you find out that you are really more gifted than you thought you were. Now, go practice!

YOUR SPIRITUAL GUIDES

There are different groups of nonphysical beings that can be called upon for guidance and protection in everyday life. Calling forth these beings and inviting them into your life is a positive way to develop your connection to the higher realms and to open your channel to receiving information and guidance from above. These beings can include angels, archangels, ascended masters, teachers, and guides. I usually encourage my clients and students simply to say, "I call forth all of my masters, teachers, guides, and angels."

Angels are beings who aid us in times of danger or illness. They have never incarnated in a body. They can look like light beings with wings and feathers, cherubs, or light forms without wings or feathers. Our subconscious mind usually dictates what an angel looks like to us. They often appear in groups, as in "a host of angels."

Archangels are angels who were sent out by God. They have no karma. These mighty angels are very present on our planet at this time. They are here to help us survive all the devastation, wars, and negativity on the planet right now. Theirs is a big job. An example of an archangel who may be familiar to you is Archangel Michael, the protector of the children of God.

Ascended masters are beings who usually have lived on this earth, but have completed their ascension. They now hold an office in the Great White Brotherhood, which is the Spiritual Hierarchy that oversees the world and our enlightenment. An example is the Master Jesus who is sometimes called Sananda.

Teachers are people who have left their bodies when they were functioning at a high mental and spiritual level. They have chosen to teach from the ethers rather than reincarnate. They choose who they will teach, as do the masters. Masters and teachers have their own areas of expertise. They choose those of us who share the same gifts and strengths.

Guides are beings who left the body and chose to help us from the other side. They differ from teachers in that they were not functioning at as high a mental or spiritual level. They often learn from us, as we learn from them.

ACCESSING MESSAGES FROM SPIRIT

There are two basic reasons for wanting to receive messages from spirit. The first is to get answers about your own life. The second is to get answers for other people, which can include doing a "psychic reading." As discussed above under "Psychic Gifts," there are several ways to receive information from your higher self and/or spiritual masters, teachers, guides, and angels. My strongest gift has been seeing, although as the years go by, I have become adept in all intuitive areas: seeing, hearing, knowing, feeling, and even smelling. This section discusses accessing information by using the various gifts.

For people who want to do readings but are unable to see psychically, accessing by hearing words or receiving mental images is also effective. In fact, in my work I use a combination of techniques: seeing the aura, listening to verbal messages from spirit, and receiving images. For example, I might ask my guidance a question about a client and receive an image or symbol. I then usually ask what the symbol means. At that point, I usually hear a response. After accessing by hearing and receiving images for a period of time, you probably will start seeing psychically as well. Then by examining auras, you will be able to verify the messages you have been receiving.

When I first started meditating, I began receiving answers and messages from spirit. I tested this accessing process by calling forth my higher self and spiritual masters. Then I asked the question, "How much will my Public Service bill be?" The answer I heard immediately was, "$260." I doubted the amount because it seemed unusually high. The next day, I received the bill in the mail and it was, in fact, $260. Of course, I was thrilled - not by the amount of the bill, but by the fact that I had gotten my first answer in a verifiable form. I then started asking many questions and receiving answers.

My next task was to trust the answers. In the beginning I was not very trusting. No one ever is. But I had to continue asking and listening and trusting in order to perfect the technique to the greatest degree of reliability. I had to give myself a chance. The more I practiced the technique of asking and listening, the more I discovered this avenue is a reliable way to the truth.

When the answers come, they usually seem like a thought in my mind rather than a different voice from the "outside." However, now and then, when information is very critical and timely, I do hear a loud male voice in my head that says, "Yes, "No," "Watch out," or "Stay clear." These are warnings. But most answers to my questions sound like a thought. One of my male clients says he gets "hunches" or intuitive "hits" about certain things. Others sometimes actually see a message printed in the mind as if a ticker tape is announcing a message.

Sometimes the messages come in the form of symbols or visions. You may be shown a picture or word; then you should ask your guidance what the symbol means. Soon you will learn to understand the symbolic language of your own subconscious and super-conscious minds. The same is true for messages received in dreams. They are usually highly symbolic, and it is important to learn what the symbols represent to you. There are many dream books on the market that can be helpful as guidelines, but they cannot replace learning to interpret and understand your own set of symbols.

When accessing messages, it is very important to discern - by the quality of the message - if it is coming from a being of high intention. You can tell this by the context and nature of the message itself. If you hear a voice telling you to harm another or to do something for a selfish purpose, obviously the source is not of the highest caliber. In fact, if you do hear such messages, this may be your negative ego talking, or you may have a nonpositive earthbound spirit or entity (if so, see "Removing Entities and Releasing Attachments" in chapter five). On the other hand, if the message is a loving, compassionate one, the source is probably of a high nature and worth listening to.

KINESIOLOGY OR MUSCLE TESTING

While you are developing your intuitive gifts and building your confidence and trust in them, a powerful technique for accessing information is kinesiology, also known as muscle testing. You have been hearing for many years now that we are affected by our thoughts and feelings about ourselves. If we are silently or outwardly expressing negative thoughts or feelings about ourselves or someone else, our subconscious mind takes it in as truth. This can become part of our belief system and, therefore, part of our reality. Because our subconscious mind works this way, we are able to find out exactly what is buried in the mind, the body, and the emotional self. There are several different ways to gain access to the subconscious belief system. Kinesiology, or muscle testing, is one of them. This technique was first introduced by author George Goodheart in his book *Applied Kinesiology*. A book that is a good reference for kinesiology is *Power vs. Force* by David R Hawkins, M.D.

Some people do their grocery shopping by muscle testing each product to find out if it is good for the body. Kinesiology is also used for determining which supplements are beneficial. In fact, it can be used to answer any number of questions about your own truth. However, be aware, your inner guidance can play tricks on you if you doubt the results. Always trust the first answer you get.

The body tests strong when the statement you make is positive or true for you; and weak when the statement is negative or not true for you. For example, "My name is Patrisha." (true) or "My name is Lucy." (not true)

Muscle Testing Another Person

There are several different methods or styles for using kinesiology. The most common is to have the person being tested raise the dominant (most used, as in right-handed) arm to shoulder level at the side of the body. The person doing the testing places a hand on the arm just above the subject's wrist. The subject is asked to push up against the tester to determine the muscle strength. To test the process, the subject is asked to make a statement, such as, "My name is Patrisha," while the tester simultaneously presses down on the arm. If the statement is true, the arm meets the pressure of the tester and does not fall. Then the subject says, "My name is Lucy" (assuming this is not her real name). In this instance the body muscles lose strength and the arm collapses under the pressure of the tester. This establishes the base strength of the person being tested. Yes, it works, even with statements like this; the subconscious knows what is true and responds accordingly.

There are several guidelines to follow to ensure the reliability of this technique:

- The person must be grounded, centered in the body, and in present time. Before beginning, have the person make a statement such as "I am grounded and centered and present in my body now." Also have the person tap the thymus to open the meridian, connecting the head and heart. However, if despite these techniques, the person tests erratically (all "yes" or all "no" responses no matter what the statement, or tests "no" to statements you both know are true), the subject is probably not present in the body. This subject needs additional grounding techniques. (See "Grounding" in chapter three.)

- Breathing is very important. The subject and tester should take deep breaths before and during the process in order to stay open, relaxed, and grounded. People stop breathing when nervous, frightened, or threatened. You cannot get an accurate reading if the subject stops breathing.

- The statements must be in present time. "This product is beneficial for me" is a statement in present time. "This product will benefit me" is a statement in future time and, thus, will not produce accurate results.

- The statements must be stated as fact. "This product is beneficial for me" is stated as a fact. "Does this product benefit me?" is stated as a question, not as a fact.

- There should be no distractions, not even music, that could influence the reactions of the subject. The muscles react to all external and internal stimuli, so there should not be any distractions that override the focus on the statements being tested.

- The tester and subject should not look at each other. The emotional connection between the two people could influence the muscle response.

- The tester should consciously magnetically pull his/her own aura in to the spine so the energy field does not influence the subject's results.
- If the issue being tested involves a product (e.g., a food item or supplement) or article (e.g., a book the subject is considering reading), the subject should hold the product next to the solar plexus while making the statement, "This (product, book, whatever) is beneficial for me."
- The statements should not be emotionally charged. Muscle testing is not reliable if the person becomes emotionally involved in the outcome. "This product is beneficial for me" is usually a simple statement that the person is not emotionally attached to. "John loves me" is an emotionally charged issue. If you do want to find answers to emotional questions, the tester can make the statements silently and test the person that way. If you are at all concerned that the emotions of the tester might influence the results, you can write the statements on pieces of paper and put each in a separate envelope. This is a double-blind test in which neither the subject nor the tester knows the issue being tested. Hold the envelope next to the subject's solar plexus and make the statement, "The statement in this envelope is true." Write the response on the outside of each envelope. Open them once the testing is completed.

MUSCLE TESTING YOURSELF

Kinesiology also can be used on yourself. There are variations with this technique, but basically you use the fingers on your hands to test your own muscle strength. In one version, take the tips of the thumb and little finger on the nondominant hand and press them together to form a circle. Then take the thumb and forefinger of the other hand and press the tips together while interlocking with the first circle. The two interlocking circles form a figure eight or two links on a chain. As the statement is made, squeeze the thumb and little finger of the nondominant hand tightly; simultaneously pull against them with the thumb and forefinger of the dominant hand. If the two "circles" come apart, the muscles tested weak and the statement is false. If the fingers stay intertwined, the statement is true.

How To Do An Intuitive (PSYCHIC) Reading

Thousands of psychics do readings for people, and there are as many styles and techniques for doing readings as there are psychics. Most people begin by using a tool such as Tarot cards, astrology charts, numerology, psychometry, aura reading, etc. Tarot cards are one of the easiest tools because the cards offer an easily learned structure for reading the client's subconscious mind. The client's subconscious mind picks the card; the predefined specific meaning of each card gives the reader a clear starting point for interpretation. Many readers gradually move beyond the tool or medium as other intuitive gifts develop through experience. The tools are very helpful for building confidence. At some point, your own intuitive will show you your own style and at this time it becomes a creative art.

In my style of reading, the first thing I do is a preparatory ritual. I close my eyes. I stretch my neck and back to open the spine to allow the energy to flow freely. Then I call forth all of my masters, teachers, guides, and angels, and I ask for the Christ protection. I also ask for my ego to step aside so my own self-interest does not distort the messages. After I am protected, I align my chakras with those of the client who sits facing me.

I use a one-hour tape to record the reading for the client. Since I become very altered during a reading or session, I use the tape as my timer. I know that half of the time is gone when it is time to turn the tape over. I also have a clock visible if I need it. Sometimes the energy gets so intense that it affects the electronics of the tape recorder.

I begin the reading by opening my eyes and scanning the client's aura. I describe what I see to the client. This takes about ten minutes. The first thing I look for is the spiritual level this person has attained in the ascension process. I quantify the amount of light, the size and resilience of the aura, the amount of the soul (part of the higher self) he/she has embodied, and the potential for embodying more of the soul in the near future. I look for this information first because the most important aspect of my work is facilitating the enlightenment or ascension process.

The second thing I look for is entities. These usually appear as humanoid-shaped forms. They can be positive and light in color (angels, guides, extraterrestrials, deceased friends or relatives) or nonpositive and dark in color (entities or demons, lizard beings, insect creatures). When I tell people about seeing deceased relatives or friends, they often cry. It is important to have a box of tissues handy. If I identify nonpositive entities, I know this is one of the most important things for me to help the client to clear after the reading is completed.

The next information I look for is general patches of darkness that can be so thick they look like sticky tar. Bright or clear colors are positive energy; dark areas or dirty colors indicate energy blockages that represent issues - the client's "stuff." Each dark area represents an issue. I look for dark red, "mucousy" green, black, or dirty yellow patches. Dark red can be rage; if it is over a body part, it can be inflammation or disease. Dirty green generally means jealousy, envy, or rigidity. Black patches are blockages from old negative habits and patterns that have not yet been resolved and eliminated. Black also can be depression that literally appears as a black cloud above the person. Dirty yellow can indicate a smoker (cigarettes or marijuana; I always ask the client which). If it is not smoke, it is polluted thoughts and emotions. With each patch of darkness, I ask my guidance what it represents. I use this information as the basis for the reading. Also, if I don't see what I'm looking for, I ask my guidance for the information and wait to receive an answer before proceeding. If no answer is immediately forthcoming, I make a mental note to go back to the area later.

The last thing I look for is the client's creative gifts or strengths. These can be either currently active or potential talents, such as music, art, technology, writing, channeling, and/or healing.

In the aura, whatever is on the right side of the body is on the way out. Things on the left are coming in. If I see negativity on the left, I take note to clear this before the client leaves. In fact, I work with the person until the aura is as clean as it can become within the one session. Following this work with the client, he/she receives an energy healing to further clear and smooth the aura.

Two good books for viewing pictures of auras are *Hands of Light* by Barbara Brennan and *The Rainbow Bridge, Phase II* by the Two Disciples.

As I observe things or beings in an aura, I describe them to the client. After the scanning is complete, I invite the client to ask questions. By the time I have scanned the aura, I have collected almost all of the information I need to answer the questions. If I don't know an answer, I ask my guidance and wait for a response. If I don't receive an answer, I tell the client I have not received any information on that issue. There can be information that the person is not supposed to know at this time. I never guess or make anything up. I may speculate, but if so, I tell the client that is what I am doing.

The scanning and questions usually take about thirty minutes. Although I am very intuitive, fortune-telling is not my forté. The emphasis of my work is helping people resolve their issues so they can experience peace, joy, abundance, and happiness. The second half of the session is spent clearing issues that were uncovered. I always ask the client what he/she wants to work on. In general, we work on two major issues per session. Many of the techniques I use for helping people clear their issues are detailed in this book.

After a session is complete, I usually hug the client and thank him/her. This is followed by a thirty to forty-five minute energy healing from one of the freelance healers who assist me.

TWO

Subtle Bodies and Chakras

SUBTLE BODIES

*t*here are several different layers to the aura, and these layers are known as bodies. Of course, everyone is familiar with the physical body because we "wear" it every day. But there are more subtle (light) bodies outside of the physical.

ETHERIC BODY

The next body extends about two inches out from the physical and is called the etheric body. This body is composed of a web of lines of light that cross each other. These crossings are called *nadis* in Sanskrit. This body is blue in color. It is the map or blueprint for the physical body. It holds impressions of all organs, glands, and meridians. Many healers can scan (feel) the etheric web and sense hot spots, cold spots, disease, scar tissue and many other disorders and/or blockages.

The hot spots can be a buildup of toxins or may be an inflamed area or organ. The cold spots can represent blocked areas where there is little blood flow or energy. An abnormal shape or bump can be something in the body that is out of alignment, such as a bone or tendon, or something that doesn't have a smooth energy flow to it.

Clairvoyant healers see the etheric body and notice red areas or dark areas where an imbalance or disease is held. The etheric body is made up of millions of beautiful strands of light that flow back and forth like blades of grass in the wind. It is very important to treat this body gently or you can tear it. It is very fragile; so when doing a healing, slow gentle movements are suggested for scanning or clearing this body. It is easier to feel with your hands what is in the aura when you move ever so slowly and gently.

Emotional Body

The second body out from the physical is the emotional body. This body can extend out as far as three feet, depending on how emotionally expressive the individual is. This body is made up of beautiful pastel colors - green, yellow, lavender, blue, pink. This body holds the emotions, such as love, fear, hate, passion.

For the most part, the emotional body lives in the past. It can be beautiful and colorful like a pastel painting; or it can be polluted with anger, hate, or other negative feelings.

When I look at a client's emotional body, I first look for the beauty of the creative energy. I can see which gifts this person has and the potential gifts not yet opened. I then take a look to see what negative blocks are overshadowing the gifts, so I will know what issues or feelings this person needs to clear so their radiance can shine through.

Mental Body

The next body out from the emotional is the mental body or mind. This is the lower mind. The higher mind is in the spiritual body and is part of the higher self. The mental body is yellow in color and holds our thoughts. When we think about something, it takes a form; thus, we have thought-forms in the mental body that can be seen by clairvoyants. Usually when a person comes directly from work for a session with me, the aura is predominantly yellow because the mind is still chattering. The color of thought is yellow. For the most part, the mental body lives in the future, asking "What if...?"

All disease and distortion in the physical body comes in by way either of the mental body or emotional body. As soon as we feel something or think about something, it takes a form and, unless we clear the negative thoughts or feelings, they can move into the physical body and settle in, causing blockage and eventually causing pain and swelling. Thoughts and feelings from the current life or past lives create all things.

Spiritual Body

Beyond the mental body lies the spiritual body. There is a whole set of higher bodies in this one, as I referred to above when I mentioned the "higher mind." However, I'll just give the basics here. The spiritual body holds our connection to the higher self, to soul, spirit, and the Godhead. Thus, the spiritual body holds our potential, creativity, great gifts, and the knowledge of our mission on the planet. By expanding yourself out, you can stretch into your higher self and access all that is there, thereby moving into your strengths and purpose.

The spiritual body is incredibly resilient and huge, radiating beautiful light that sends out beams in all directions. A person who has expanded out into their spiritual body, and functions from this level, radiates great light. Others can feel this light. For instance, when you are powerful and expand your aura, others will turn around when you walk into a room because they feel your light first - before they see your face. And the projection you send out will be responded to. If you smile, you will receive a smile back. And yes, this will happen most times anyway, but more so if you are clear and loving in your powerful aura. This is why it is important to function from the heart. If you are working on expanding into your spiritual self, you will become more and more powerful, and it is important that the energy you radiate is love.

CHAKRAS

There are numerous books on the subject of chakras. Almost everyone who writes of metaphysical matters discusses chakras at one point or another. It is difficult to find any two sources that completely agree on this subject. Most systems speak of the seven physical body chakras, although some delineate only six. Even those who agree on the number, disagree about where they are located. Some systems speak of the seven physical body chakras plus other etheric body chakras. These systems become even more divergent, with the number of chakras varying from twelve to literally thousands.

Everyone seems to agree that the chakras are energy centers that connect the physical body to spirit. They also seem to agree that each chakra relates to specific body organs or systems, and that each chakra has its related emotional and mental issues. However, the various sources do not always agree on which body parts are controlled by which chakra, nor on which emotional/mental issues correspond with which chakra. Bearing this in mind, I will present my understanding of chakras and their related physical, emotional, mental, and spiritual issues.

A chakra is a cone-shaped wheel of spinning energy in the aura. Chakras occur in pairs, one in the front of the body and one in the back. Their points meet within the spine. This point is where most of the debris, blockages, and memories from the current and past lives are stored. When I look at an aura, I see seven major physical body chakras:

- First   Base/Root Chakra
- Second   Sacral Chakra
- Third   Solar Plexus Chakra
- Fourth   Heart Chakra
- Fifth   Throat Chakra
- Sixth   Third Eye Chakra
- Seventh Crown Chakra.

Each chakra has its own purpose. I'll give an example. If a person has a heart attack, the heart organ is connected to the energy vortex of the heart chakra. A heart attack is caused literally by a broken heart. In fact, when I look at the heart chakra of someone with heart disease or problems, it is usually torn or weak and limp. So when analyzing different disorders or diseases, I always take a look at the associated chakra.

First Chakra

The first/base/root chakra is red, which is a grounding color. It is full of courage, vitality, and self-confidence.

It stimulates life energy and helps build inner strength, security, and will power. It also holds physical power and the gifts of levitation, teleportation, and bilocation. It is a survival chakra. Its negative aspects include anger and the feeling "I'm wrong."

The endocrine glands associated with this chakra are the reproductive glands. The base chakra governs the reproductive system, sexual organs, legs and feet, tailbone, colon, and spinal column.

The base chakra is our connection to the earth. It is masculine in nature. A masculine chakra is dynamic and emits energy. This chakra is concerned with physical-body issues and is the source of physical manifestation. This chakra contains the kundalini energy. It is the grounding chakra. Spacey people who are not grounded (see "Grounding," chapter three) are out of their bodies a lot because of fear or habit. They generally aren't consciously connected to this chakra much of the time. If a person is not connected to the first chakra, he/she cannot be connected to the body, or to the earth. This person generally is avoiding being present on the planet and often avoids feeling and facing base-chakra issues of fear and survival. Until we accept our humanness and stay present in our body, we cannot anchor our higher self into ourself or on the planet. This means we cannot continue to evolve in the ascension process.

SECOND CHAKRA

The second/sacral chakra is orange in color. It is the polarity chakra, the balance between masculine and feminine. It is the creativity chakra with artistic energy. The emotional body connects to this chakra. This chakra is also a power chakra because this is the area where the *hara* exists. The *hara* is our center of power. It is an essence that can be the size of a pea and inactive or the size of a basketball when developed and active. The *hara* is located two inches below the navel and two inches in. This is what yogis are referring to when they say, "Meditate on your navel." An exercise for strengthening the hara is to breathe into it. Visualize that the hara becomes larger and more resilient with each breath. The negative aspects of this chakra can be hostility, addictions and codependency, refusing to accept responsibility for one's own life, distrust, jealousy and envy, masculine-feminine imbalance, abuse of power, and sexual dysfunction.

This chakra is feminine in nature. A feminine chakra is receptive and draws energy inward. The endocrine gland usually associated with this chakra is the adrenal glands. This chakra governs the spleen, kidneys, and urinary organs.

THIRD CHAKRA

The third/solar plexus chakra is yellow in color and connects us to the mental body. It holds self-confidence and determination on the positive side, and we can make things happen from here. This chakra holds wisdom, clarity (clear thoughts), self-esteem, happiness, and curiosity. It is feminine in nature. This is also a power chakra. However, because this chakra is also an ego center, it expresses the power of our will, unworthiness, and the need to be first or best; our competitive side comes out here. It also holds fear and control issues, rage, and anger.

The endocrine gland usually associated with this chakra is the pancreas. The third chakra governs the stomach, liver, pancreas, gall bladder, intestines, sympathetic nervous system, blood sugar, and digestive system.

Keeping the first, second, and third chakras open is vitally important for our sexuality. Many spiritual people have stopped having sex for three reasons: (1) They believe they have to remain celibate to be spiritual and/or they choose to use the sexual energy to fuel their enlightenment; (2) They lack sexual hormones; and/or (3) They begin living out of the higher chakras, not allowing energy to move through and stimulate the first, second, and third chakras, thereby not allowing sexual feelings in the body.

If the first chakra is closed, the person is not grounded and therefore is not in the body to feel or respond to sexual desire. If the second chakra is closed, there is no sexual desire. If the third chakra is closed, the person cannot feel emotion. Also, many women are non-orgasmic for fear of giving their power away, because the orgasm is the most vulnerable state for a woman to be in. Usually the dissatisfaction from lack of orgasm through sexuality with a partner continues because there is no give or take or interchange of pleasurable energy. Thus, masturbation is usually common because it is safer to have sex with yourself than seemingly to give away your power and control to another. So, these people are usually frustrated. In actuality the orgasm is the gift to the self. It is not necessarily giving anything away. It is a sharing of energies with your partner for your benefit and his or hers.

In our new spiritual way of thinking, we must take into consideration the pros and cons of sharing sexual energy with another person. First of all, we have hooked a cord of energetic connection into all of the sexual partners we have been with in our lifetime. This means that when we are having sex without first disconnecting these cords, we can be energetically connected with everybody that we and our partner have had sex with throughout our lives. This is especially true if one or both are motivated only by lust and desire. If your partner is not clear, you are running his/her negative energy through your body. Obviously, it is wise to choose a consciously spiritual mate or partner whose intent is love. Otherwise, negative energy weaves its way up through all the chakras. In other words, casual or recreational sex can be quite harmful. So, be very selective and honor your godself as your intent while making love. You honor yourself by choosing a spiritually-oriented partner who loves and honors you.

Fourth Chakra

The fourth chakra is the heart chakra. Historically, it has been green in color. However, as people advance on the spiritual path of enlightenment, I am now seeing a core light of rosy-pink beginning to emerge in the center of this chakra. Rose is the color of universal love, as opposed to self-love. In this transformation with the rose blending with the green - which has been the color of balance, harmony, healing and growth - we are now experiencing more love, kindness, consideration for others, and the desire to serve humankind and the planet as a whole. Love is held in the heart chakra. It connects us to our unconditional love. Also in this chakra are our productivity, enthusiasm, playfulness, and sense of peace.

On the negative side, we harbor resentments, the feeling "I'm not good enough," and other feelings of inferiority. Also, heart issues can include the inability to change ourself, attachment to material objects, and feelings of jealousy, greed and envy. This chakra is masculine in nature.

The endocrine gland usually associated with the heart chakra is the thymus. This chakra governs the heart, thymus, lungs, lymph, immune system, circulatory system, arms, and hands.

High Heart Chakra

The high heart or thymus chakra is a new chakra

now being recognized. It is turquoise in color, combining blue and green energies. This connects us to our expression, confidence, and positive warrior nature. It appears to function as an interface between the heart and throat chakras, and it houses the ability to speak our own truth. This also helps to build the immune system. It blends masculine and feminine together equally through expression so each gender may speak its own truth. Some people are adding this chakra to the seven-chakra system making it an eight-chakra system, but I will not for the sake of keeping things simple.

Fifth Chakra

The fifth/throat chakra is blue in color. It is the avenue of expression, including the expression of creativity, the ability to sing, and speaking our mind. Other positive aspects of this chakra include the connection to spiritual thought and knowledge. It is also the hormonal balancer and, therefore, is a key to good health.

The negative aspects include judgment of self and others, bull-headedness, and rigidity. The beliefs "I'm undeserving" and "I'm unlovable" are held in the fifth chakra. Rage is also held in this area and the jaw is affected. In fact, a tight jaw usually means the person is holding anger. Screaming into a pillow is good therapy for clearing this area. This chakra is a problem area for women who haven't been able to express their opinions. The outer neck sometimes appears red or blotchy when unexpressed feelings are held inside. This chakra is feminine in nature. It connects to the causal body, which holds our karma.

The endocrine gland usually associated with the fifth chakra is the thyroid. This chakra governs the thyroid, parathyroid, throat, jaw, neck, and mouth.

SIXTH CHAKRA

The sixth chakra is the third eye. It is indigo in color. This is the center of intuition, mysticism, imagination, psychic powers, understanding, and dream activity. When we astral travel, this is the chakra we leave from, connected by the silver cord. From this area we access information or messages from our higher self or the superconscious, including our guides and angels. We also formulate visions from this area and are able to comprehend information coming from higher levels (i.e., other dimensions and realms).

On the negative side, this chakra holds antagonism, confusion, insecurity, and fear of others; this can result in isolation and reclusive behavior, often rationalized as "being spiritual."

There is no masculine or feminine nature associated with the sixth or seventh chakras because they are a higher expression.

The endocrine gland usually associated with the sixth chakra is the pituitary. This chakra governs the pituitary gland, hypothalamus, lower brain, and central nervous system.

SEVENTH CHAKRA

The seventh/crown chakra is violet in color. It connects us to the higher self. On the positive side, it holds purity of thoughts and feelings, artistic talent and creativity, and high ideals. It is here that we experience serenity, joy, and gratitude.

On the negative side, this chakra holds beliefs such as "life is a struggle" and feelings of overwhelm and being overlooked. It also holds selfishness and ill intentions. A person blocked in this chakra often wants his/her problems to be magically resolved without any effort on his/her part.

Because this chakra sits on top of the head, it's not surprising to know that if this chakra is blocked we can experience a headache. A slight swirling with the flat of your hand in a clockwise manner, about four inches above your head, will open this channel to God and allow trapped energy out, thereby relieving the pain.

The endocrine gland usually associated with this chakra is the pineal. This chakra governs the pineal, upper brain, and central nervous system.

This completes the discussion of the seven major physical body chakras plus the new high heart/thymus chakra. There are also minor physical body chakras, including the liver chakra, spleen chakra, hand chakras, and feet chakras.

Nonphysical Chakras

Beyond the physical body, there are additional etheric chakras in the aura. As mentioned earlier, most sources disagree as to the number and location of these. They appear to me only in the auras of clients who are advanced on the spiritual path. When they do appear, I see five additional chakras - the eighth, ninth, tenth, eleventh, and twelfth, located above the head. To me these upper chakras appear as "plates" or flat discs of light. Two additional chakras often mentioned in the literature are the Alpha and Omega. When these appear to me, they look like spheres containing constantly undulating waves of light. These etheric chakras function differently than the physical-body chakras. They are regulators of light and play a vital role in the formation of the lightbody, which is discussed with "ascension" in chapter nine.

THREE

Hands-on Healing

*h*ealing is such an expansive word. There are many levels involved. The word itself means that a problem, wound, disease, or emotional disorder is improving. In the physical body it often means that damaged tissue is now receiving appropriate blood supply and is mending and becoming elastic. But is the problem only physical? Perhaps the wound is in one of the other subtle bodies, like the emotional body, mental body, or spiritual body. What happens then? The same thing, except that in the emotional body the feeling is being healed, in the mental body the thought is being healed, in the spiritual body the essence is being healed. Of course, the spiritual level is the higher self and the issues have to do with one's godness.

We all have core level issues that were probably brought into this life by soul to be healed. The list of core level issues is infinite; there are as many issues as there are people. We each have our own. For example, a core issue may be an identity issue, such as "Who am I really?" "What is my purpose on this planet in this life?" Or perhaps you wish you had been the opposite gender. Or maybe the issue is abandonment because you feel you that were not wanted by your parents, or perhaps separation from God. Interestingly, it has been my experience that we often have the same core level issues as our family, though perhaps in a different order of importance. However, the issues can be different within a family. One person may not be able to make a living due to low self-esteem and not feeling he/she deserves abundance; while another family member may have the capacity to manifest abundance. Why is this? Probably because the manifesting person cleared the issue of "lack" in a past incarnation and is working on clearing a different issue in this life.

We have to address our core belief to complete our healing process. We can heal the physical, emotional, or mental bodies; but if we don't get to our core level issues, our problems may return or new problems may develop. Limiting beliefs are strung together like a ball of yarn; we have to unwind it until the ball is gone. Many issues have several levels and sub-levels. The various levels sometimes seem the same, and you may say, "But I already cleared that issue!" Well guess what, you cleared a layer of it, but more lies waiting. The healing process calls for patience. It may take years or lifetimes to clear one major issue. Deep healing can be done in one lifetime, but it takes a tremendous amount of courage and determination to do this. You must be goal-oriented, and dedicated to the enlightenment process, to stick with it.

Another reason the healing process requires patience is because there is a period of integration for changes. You can make a huge realization, the light goes on, and you say, "Ah ha!" or "Oh my gosh, I got it!" and the old program can begin to break down. This creates a gap and opens a space for the magic of growth to happen. The space can be filled by the new way of viewing yourself and living your life. At first this space can feel like a void or emptiness. You can experience a feeling of depression or hopelessness between the old way of doing things and the new. Just remember that this void is fertile ground in which to plant new positive seeds for a new and positive way of living. Another thing I have realized through the years is that the more painful something is on the "dark" side of growth, the greater the rewards on the "light" side.

One of the side-effects of healing is something I call "burning." This means burning away or dissolving negativity, toxins, and/or karma. Sometimes this process is uncomfortable. Some symptoms of "burning" are irritability, rage, over-sensitivity, sadness, depression, crying, grieving, flashbacks of old memories surfacing as they are being released, and hot flashes that can last for days. If the symptoms become severe, you can have what is known as a healing crisis and become physically ill, often with flu symptoms such as diarrhea, colds, body aches, and/or hot or cold sweats. Sometimes dormant diseases surface as they are being released. This can result in symptoms of a particular disease. A good example is the bout of hepatitis I experienced after being in the presence of Sai Baba. The disease had been dormant in my body for twenty years (see "Kundalini," chapter eight). If you find yourself in a healing crisis, get some healing work or a massage and stay in bed and drink plenty of fluids. Know that your body is releasing old disease. Say goodbye to it all!

IMPLANTS

Implants can be found in the aura of many people. They may have been there for thousands of lifetimes. The most common implant is a lance, or knife, or other weapon, because the aura can create a form or impression of the object that killed the person in a previous life. When the etheric body goes back into the soul after death, it can take memories with it. If the memory from one lifetime was traumatic enough, that memory can stay in the atomic structure for millions of years and continue to reform scar tissue over and over in the fibers of the etheric body of other incarnations. So if you are in a healing situation, feeling someone's aura, and you detect an object that feels like metal, it might be.

I had a relevant experience happen to me several years ago. It did not involve an implant, but it did involve a past-life memory carried forth in my aura. I was hosting a party for healers and two different healers asked if one of my legs was crippled. I said no, and they were both surprised. They both intuitively had seen a past life, and I still had the impression of a shriveled up and crippled leg in my energy field. They both did some healing on me and the etheric body was returned to health. My mind was healed as well, because deep within it had been the memory of this condition.

There also may be implants that feel like spaghetti or snakes or even little creatures called "harpies." Harpies live in peoples aura's in a nest. Sometimes they bite because they have teeth.

Another form of implant is a device used to control a person. Before the civilization of Atlantis, there was a small continent called Lemuria. The people on this continent were small with brown skin. These people were pure of heart and incredibly loving. However, they were at one time attacked by some beings called the Electrical Ones (or other names) who came from a different universe. These beings were cruel and controlling and took over the Lemurians. They implanted metal devices in anyone who wouldn't do as they were told. Women were often implanted in the uterus; men were usually implanted behind the ear. The devices were used to zap the person with electricity to control their behavior. The war of the Lemurians and this other species lasted only about 500 years, but it was not uncommon for the Lemurians to be killed and reincarnate back into a body immediately to save the others, only to be killed again. This experience established a pattern of automatic "defend and attack" which many of us still carry. An example is a person today who is very defensive and will argue with you about anything. The cellular memory is still in that person and every adversarial situation triggers a need to fight for life. Remember, the etheric body is a blueprint for the physical, so the memory is in the aura. All implants can be removed by pulling them out of the aura. In fact, I have heard that there is now documentation of implants being surgically removed by medical doctors. However, I haven't seen any proof of this.

COLOR HEALING

Color Healing is fabulous because you can get creative while working on someone. I'll go through some of the colors and their uses and vibrations. These are the colors of the seven rays, which are the vibrations of creation in this dimension. The order of the colors does not correspond directly to the colors of the seven chakras, and each is less dense in vibration than the previous one.

- The densest color is red. Red is the color of divine will. It is a very basic color with a lot of energy. It is the color of passion, action, and appetite. This color stimulates you into action and you can go a long way if you have an aura full of red. Red is used in restaurants on walls and tablecloths, etc., to increase business. The appetite is stimulated and you eat more and faster and out you go!

- The next color in density is blue. This color is the love and wisdom vibration. It is the color of peace. It can also be cooling or even menthol in feeling, depending on the shade; the lighter shade is the cool waves of menthol. It is also the color of the etheric body.

- Yellow vibrates at the level of the mind, concrete intelligence. Yellow is the color of thought and creativity. This color is also wonderful to use to brighten up the aura.

- Green is the color of the heart chakra; so, obviously, love is one of the characteristics of this color. It is also the color of wealth, health, balance, and harmony. If you want to feel fresh and healthy, wear green.

- Orange is the vibration of high thinkers. It is also the color of sacrifice and is often worn by saints, gurus, and monks. It is a highly vibrant, holy color. Inventors and other creative people, such as actors, often have this color in the aura.

- Indigo is the color of devotion. It is the meditative state. Calm, peacefulness, and insight are commonly found in this color.

- The last color, with the least dense vibration, is lavender. This color is very magical. It is used to transmute nonpositive into positive. It is used in magic, ceremony, and ritual. Lavender has an antiseptic action; by visually pouring lavender into the aura (i.e., using your imagination) you can remove infections, etc. But don't use too much of this color or it will start to itch!

By using these colors you can create positive changes. Use your intent and visualize adding one or more of these colors to the aura and/or body of your client or friend. Let your intuition guide you. You can experiment using different colors, then feel the aura and notice the difference. Also, ask your client what he/she is feeling. And, of course, as soon as you are able to use your spiritual "sight," you will be able to see the changes for yourself.

There's one thing to remember: As soon as you think of a color to use, you must only think about that color for a second or so, because as soon as the mind gets hold of the color it will turn it yellow. Remember, yellow is the color of the mind/mental body.

TONING

Toning is a very beneficial technique to use when doing a healing. Toning is exactly what it sounds like: you make sounds with your mouth to shake loose dense matter from a person's aura or body and to raise the vibration. Stand over the person and direct a tone into the blocked area. You may need to put your hands up to your mouth like you are going to yell, in order to direct the tone into the body. This may sound odd, but sometimes this is the only way to clear a person. The sound that comes out of you may scare you a little because sometimes the sound needs to be very deep, or high, or raspy, depending on how much power and/or what vibration is needed. If you feel embarrassed to try this, just stand in the shower and practice. Make very high and eerie sounds; then tone very low. Feel the effect on your body. Do know that while you are doing a healing on a person, you have your guidance and the person's guidance around you and they send the appropriate energy through the sound.

GROUNDING

To be grounded means your consciousness is focused in your body. You are not grounded when you are in an altered state, or you feel spacey or absent-minded. It is important to be grounded to function properly in every day life. You need to be fully present and attentive while driving in order to avoid accidents. You need to be grounded and fully present while accomplishing tasks, to focus on the details and know what you have done and what needs to be done to complete a task. When talking with others, you need to be grounded to remember what was said between you. If you are often forgetful or lose things or don't remember telling people the things they say you did, you probably are not in your body. You are probably not grounded. This is a form of escape from feelings, from responsibility, and from life. It also can be a defense mechanism for escaping trauma. Some people left their bodies at a very early age due to a trauma or repeated traumas and have not been able return.

It is normal to be ungrounded some of them time; everyone daydreams. However, this can become a serious problem that affects the ability to function reliably and responsibly in life. When carried to an extreme, this state becomes definable as mental illness. Some people can be diagnosed as schizophrenic, bipolar, or with another emotional or mental disorder; but a large part of the real problem may be that the person is not grounded.

As discussed below in the section on entities, many times "mentally ill" people also house nonpositive entities. One of the most common symptoms is hearing voices. These voices can be from the entity(s). One of the many consequences of not being grounded is that the aura becomes expanded and vulnerable, so entities have easy access. In my work, I have counseled many people who had been diagnosed with mental disorders. My first action is to teach them to get back in the body and stay grounded. I have them practice the techniques given below several times each day. The second step is to look at the aura and identify, then remove, any nonpositive entities. The third step is to seal the aura to ensure that it becomes a protective pink bubble.

I have found in many cases that once a client is grounded and present, with entities removed, the disorder diminishes greatly and, in some cases, completely disappears. At that point, the treatment becomes comprehensive training in the routines of daily life: how to communicate with people, personal hygiene, dating, dressing appropriately, healthy eating, etc. Many of these clients have been "gone" for so long that they lost these skills or never learned them at all. Once grounded and retrained in basic life skills, many of these clients are able then to taper off and finally eliminate medications on the advice of their psychiatrists.

Grounding Techniques

Various visualizations to help you ground:
- Stand with your feet flat on the floor and your knees bent. Send energy down into the earth, then deeper and deeper. Your legs will feel heavier and heavier.
- Imagine that you are a monkey. Send your tail deep into the earth and hook it around something down there.
- Imagine tubes going straight down from the bottom of your feet deep into the earth.
- Imagine that you are a tree and you are sending roots down, deep into the earth.
- Imagine walking on wet grass with bare feet (or better

still, actually go out and do it.)

Physical actions to help you ground:
- Stand near a wall with one foot forward and one back. Lean against the wall with your arms, and push against the wall with your arms, while pushing your feet into the floor. Then switch legs.
  - Have someone push down on your shoulders.
  - Eat heavy foods (protein, grains).
  - Drink water.
  - Tap the thymus gland about ten times (located in the chest under the sternum between the heart and throat chakras).
  - Put your hands in cold water.
  - Walk outside on the ground.

PROTECTION

It is very important to protect yourself. You don't want to absorb other people's negative emotions. Nor do you want to be susceptible to the bacteria and germs that are everywhere. You also don't want to allow nonpositive entities access into your aura. The best way to be protected is to have a strong, resilient aura.

As you clear your traumatic past and present life issues; improve your mental, emotional, and physical health; and raise your vibrational level, the aura strengthens automatically and nothing of a lower, unhealthy vibration can get in. However, it can take years to build a strong aura and lightbody. Anytime you are sick or experience an emotional trauma, your aura can become weakened or even torn. Therefore, following are techniques to help you augment and strengthen your energy field until it is self-sustaining.

Protection Techniques

Some of my favorite ways to protect yourself:
- Call forth the Christ light and ask to be surrounded and protected by this white light. I do this several times a day, especially before working with any person or going into a place that may have negative energy.

- Visualize yourself surrounded by a bubble of protection, like a Christmas-tree bulb. Gold or silver are good colors to visualize around yourself. When you are wearing this "bulb," anything negative will hit the ball of light and be reflected back to its source. This is a mirroring effect.

- Call forth the Lords of Karma and ask them to send down the divine shield to surround and protect you. Simply say, "I call forth the Lords of Karma and ask you to surround and protect me with the divine shield now." Sometimes you can actually feel or hear the shield "clunk" into place around you.

- Call forth the archangels, such as Michael, Gabriel, Raphael or Ariel, and ask them for protection. You can call forth any master or divine being you choose.

How Not to Absorb Other People's Negativity

Many of us would love to be great healers and heal everyone and the planet. Although the intention is loving, many healers forget or don't know how to protect themselves from taking on other people's negative programs, feelings, thoughts, or diseases. As a personal example, years ago I went to see a psychic surgeon who could see into my body. While working on me, she found a mass of negative energy in my solar plexus chakra. At the time, I was a healer myself, working on several clients each day. The mass removed from my chakra was not even mine. I had removed negative energy from a client. Instead of releasing it to spirit, I had empathically absorbed it into my own energy system! The healer who was working on me warned me against healing this way and predicted that if I didn't stop absorbing other people's negativity into my solar plexus, I eventually would develop serious digestive problems. I did not believe her. I ignored her advice. Subsequently, I developed serious digestive problems that are mostly, but not completely, healed today. I now know that it is much harder to remove foreign negativity that came from someone else than it is to remove our own negativity. The message here is that healers may think they are helping others by taking negativity into their own body, but the consequences are serious and can be fatal to the healer.

The way I worked as a healer before was to feel the client's issues or pain in my own body, then work on them until the pain was gone in my body. This is called empathic healing. In reality, I was feeling their pain and taking it into my body as I removed it from theirs. Highly evolved beings, such as saints and gurus, can heal this way because they have the power to transmute and transform the negativity once it is in their body. However, very few of us are at that level.

The reason some people become empathic healers is because they are empathic by nature. This means they are very emotional and sensitive, usually have a large aura, and generally identify with and feel other people's pain. This is not an issue of good or bad, right or wrong; instead, it is something to be aware of and protect against - in crowds and in healing situations.

While healing a person, it is imperative to protect yourself from his/her negativity. In addition to using one or more of the techniques listed above, before doing a hands-on healing, visualize blocking your own wrists so the negative energy can't move up into your body. Also, when pulling negativity out of a person, consciously hand it to your "spiritual healing team" for removal and transmutation. All healers have their own spiritual healing "team" that guides and assists with the work. The "team" usually consists of spiritual guides, angels, and other nonphysical beings. Know that your team is with you and you can call on them for help.

DEMONSTRATION OF HANDS-ON HEALING

Have the person remove his/her shoes, belt, and jewelry, and lie on a massage table in a comfortable position, with a pillow under the knees to relax the back. The healing can be done with the person lying on the floor, but this is uncomfortable for the healer. It also can be done on a bed, but this limits access to all sides of the body. A massage table is the most comfortable and convenient. The following instructions are given as though the person is lying face-up on a table.

Call forth protection and guidance. Stand beside the person, close your eyes, and ask to be protected. You can use any of the protection techniques in the "Protection" section above, or create your own. Then call forth all of your and the person's masters, teachers, guides, angels, and soul.

Gather information. Begin by scanning the body. Place your hands over the person about six inches above the body. Keep your hands parallel with the body. Begin to move your hands slowly from head to toe, feeling for abnormalities, such as hot areas, cold spots, the absence of energy and/or jagged or overly active energy. Make a mental note of your findings. Then stand behind the head.

Begin by sending a figure-eight violet flame into the person's third eye from your third eye. Tune into the person with your most sensitive self and listen for messages from the person's soul/higher self. Trust anything intuitive that you get and add this information to the impressions you gathered during the scanning.

Massage to relax person. Use a lotion or cream and massage the neck and temples to relax the person. Then massage the person's hands and feet. Some people do not like to have their feet massaged, so always ask permission.

Prepare for chelation technique. Stand at the foot of the table and place your hands on the bottoms of the person's feet. Breath deeply while visualizing sending a tube from the base of your spine down through your own legs and feet and deep into the earth. Imagine pulling hot molten lava energy up from the center of the earth (imagine standing on top of a volcano). Bring this hot energy all the way up through your body and down through your arms and into the person's feet. You also can purse your lips as if blowing out a candle; blow the energy down your arms into the person's feet by actually blowing out small amounts of air.

Now, visualize sending a tube out the top of your head (crown chakra) and into the spiritual plane - as high as you can send it. Pull the cool rays of the moon down into your body and through your arms and hands. You will be merging the hot energy from the core of the earth (Shiva) with the cool rays of the moon from the heavens (Shakti). The cool menthol Shakti energy is light blue in color and is calming and healing. The hot Shiva energy is either red or golden or both; the hot energy is beneficial for burning out blockages and stimulating energy. Send both the cool and the hot energy into the person's feet.

Start swirling your own chakras open, starting at the base chakra. Imagine that you are lying on your back looking up at the base of your spine and with your higher will, swirl this chakra clockwise; remember that the chakras look like a megaphone that is flat on the end. Continue breathing and move up to your second chakra in front of the pelvic area; breath and swirl this chakra open in a clockwise motion (as if you were standing in front of yourself looking at a megaphone). Then do the same for the back of the second chakra. Continue this clockwise swirling and opening of all your own chakras: solar plexus, heart, throat, third eye, and crown. All this time, continue breathing and bringing energy into your own body through your base and crown chakras.

Chelation. You have been standing with the flat of your hands on the bottom of the person's feet during this preparation process, channeling energy into them. Now you will begin moving your hands up the body in a pattern that connects the chakras (there are minor chakras in the feet, ankles, knees, hips, hands, elbows, and shoulders). The positions are described below. Your hands should be gently touching the body, unless otherwise specified. This form of healing also can be done with the hands placed two inches above the body. Some people don't like to be touched.

At each position, channel energy into the body through your hands. Spend a few minutes in each position. You may feel a pulse between your hands when the energy connection has been made. If you don't feel a pulse, use your intuition to determine how long to hold each position. As you move from position to position up the chakras, always keep one hand on the body; the person may feel disconnected if you remove both hands at the same time.

There are several different ways to do chelation. The following describes one method. As you become more experienced, you will learn to use your intuition and be creative.

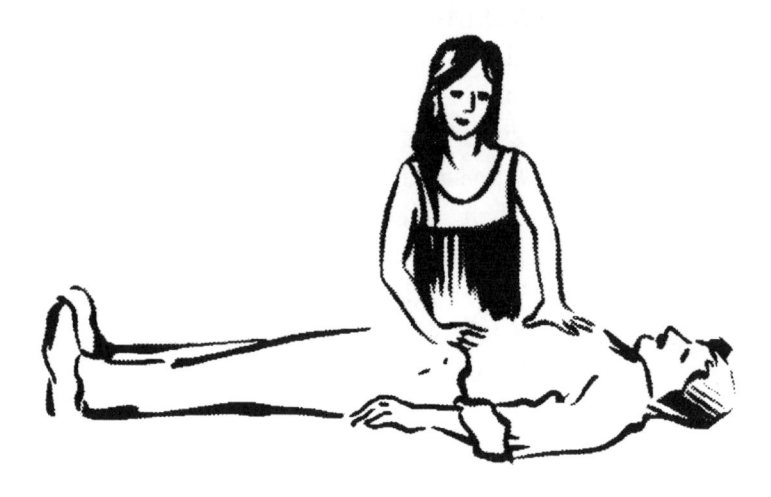

- After having your hands on the bottom of the feet, you will move to the person's right side and place your hands on top of the ankles (remember to move one hand at a time). Your left hand should be on the leg closest to you. Hold this position to connect the energy between the ankles.

- Move your left hand up to the knee on the leg closest to you. Then move the right hand to the other knee. Hold this position.

- Move the left hand to the thigh/hip of the leg closest to you (i.e., to the area where the leg meets with the trunk of the body). Then move your right hand to the other thigh/hip. Hold this position.

- Move your right hand to the bottom of the foot on the leg closest to you. At this point you have both hands on the leg closest to you and are running energy up and down this leg. Hold this position.

- Now you will cross-connect the two sides of the body. Move your right hand to the bottom of the opposite foot while keeping your left hand on the thigh/hip of the leg closest to you. Hold this position.
- Move your left hand to the other thigh/hip. At this point you have both hands on the leg farthest from you so you are running energy up and down that leg. Hold this position.
- Now, complete the cross connection of the two sides of the body by moving your right hand back to the foot closest to you. Your left hand remains on the opposite thigh/hip. Hold this position.
- Now you are ready to connect the major chakras. To connect the first and second chakras, place your left hand on the second chakra below the belly button. Hold your right hand a few inches below the base chakra (about mid-thigh), not touching the body. Depending upon how far apart the person's legs are, your hand should be between the legs but slightly above the body. Hold this position.
- Now connect the second and third chakras. First, move your right hand up and under your left hand on the person's second chakra. Your right hand will be directly under your right hand so you can channel energy from both hands into the pelvic area. Then move your left hand to the solar plexus chakra (stomach). Now you have one hand on the second chakra and one on the third. Hold this position.
- Now connect the person's solar plexus and heart chakras. Again, begin by moving your right hand underneath your left hand so both of your hands are channeling energy into the person's solar plexus. Move your left hand to the middle of the person's chest between the breasts. For a woman it is best to turn the left hand sideways (i.e., point the fingers toward the feet). At this point you have one

hand on the third chakra, and one hand on the fourth. Hold this position.

- Now connect the person's heart and throat chakras. Begin by moving your right hand underneath your left hand on the heart chakra. For a woman it is best to also turn the right hand sideways, this time with the fingers pointing towards the throat chakra. Your hands will be pointing in opposite directions as you channel energy from both of them into the chest area. Now move your left hand to the back of the person's throat chakra (i.e., under the neck). After you have connected the heart to the back of the throat, place your right hand very gently on the front of the throat chakra. At this point both of your hands will be on the front and back of the person's throat. Barely touch the front of the throat because some people become frightened if they have been choked or strangled in past or present lifetimes. Hold this position.

- At this point, move to stand at the head of the massage table, facing the top of the person's head. Move your hands one at a time to the person's shoulders and hold this position while channeling energy all the way down the person's arms and body until you feel, sense, or see the energy moving out through the feet.

- Now put your hands on the sides of the person's face (i.e., cup your hands on their cheeks in front of the ears with your fingers pointing toward the feet). Hold this position and fill the head with light.

- Finally, place both of your hands on the top of the person's head at the crown chakra and hold this position while sending energy down through the person's body.

Remember, these positions and movements are only one way to do chelation. Be creative. Let your intuition guide you. For example, at any time you can have one hand on a chakra on the front of the body and put your other hand underneath the body on the back of the chakra.

Remove Any Remaining Negative Energy. Re-scan the person's body, remembering where the problem areas were; most of these will have been corrected, but you may find areas that still need clearing. If you do locate an area that still feels congested, you can pull any negativity out with your hands. Imagine that you are growing very long fingers energetically, sending light out the tips of your fingers - about six inches. With these long fingers of light, dip into the congested area, gather up the negative energy with both hands, and pull that energy out slowly. Hand it to spirit, asking that it be purified. Do not drop the energy onto the person or into your own aura.

The material you will be pulling out may be inflammation and feel hot; or it could be an etheric implant or anything that has been in the aura as a memory. Sometimes after a person has had a tumor removed surgically, that tumor still could be in the etheric body; unless it is removed from the aura, it could materialize again in the physical body tissues. All disease moves in from the more subtle bodies into the dense, physical body. It moves from the outside in.

Continue to pull the nonpositive energy out until you cannot feel it any longer. Then swirl the person's aura (clockwise) above the opening from which you have been pulling negative energy. This closes and reseals the aura. Move to another area, if necessary, and repeat the process until you are finished. Scan one final time.

Complete the healing. Disconnect your figure-eight violet flame from between your third eye and the person's third eye. Swirl your hands clockwise above the person's body to smooth and seal the aura. When the healing is complete, push (ground) the person back into his/her body, because he/she will be floating above the physical body. Place both of your hands several feet above the person's body and gently "push" him/her back into the body. Sometimes the person will not want to go back in (it feels so good to be out!). In this case, shake the person's aura gently back and forth, so he/she will drop back into the physical body. Go to the top or crown of the head and "push" him/her back in; then to the feet and do the same.

Thank this person for allowing you to perform a healing. Remember, you didn't do it. You facilitated, as a channel for the healing, guided by spirit. You received a healing also at the same time. Thank all of the guidance who participated.

Ask the person to roll over slowly onto his/her side and slowly sit up. The person may be light-headed, so help him/her off the table. I have seen people fall forward because they were so altered. If the person needs further grounding, help with the grounding exercises listed above.

As soon as you can, wash your own face, neck, and hands - with the intent of removing any of the person's negativity. Shower when you get home, or as soon after the healing as you can.

ABSENTEE HEALING

Now that you have read the hands-on healing information, we will talk about absentee or distant healing. Absentee healing is exactly what it sounds like: it is doing a healing for someone who is not physically with you. You use the same techniques as in hands-on healing, except you visualize or imagine performing the healing rather than physically doing it. Most people are very surprised that changes and healing can happen when you use your imagination and intent to heal another person. This is a wonderful gift to give someone, especially if he/she is on the other side of the continent or the world. This is also a precious gift to give someone if you have nothing else to give. You will know inside that you have given something special to this person.

The first step in doing an absentee healing is to call forth all of your masters, teachers, guides, and angels for assistance and protection. Then call forth the person to be healed and ask his/her soul if you have permission to do the work. It is never appropriate to work on someone without the soul's consent. Ninety-nine percent of the time you will get a "yes." In fact, souls are usually thrilled that you are doing this for the personality. When you ask the person's soul for permission you may hear a "yes" or a "no." Or, you may feel a "yes" (very calm, welcoming energy) or a "no" (a jolt through your body or a very strong feeling that you are to stop). There usually is no mistaking a "no" because spirit is very emphatic if you are not to work on the person. If you get a "no," this should be respected. The person may not be ready to be healed, or you may not be the one meant to facilitate the healing. If you are not sure whether you got a "yes" or a "no" from the soul, go ahead and begin the process. If the answer was "no," you will have trouble connecting with the person or accessing any information from him/her. So just give love. If you do receive a "no," you can always try again at a later date to see if the situation has changed.

When you get permission to do the absentee healing on someone, the next step is to imagine calling forth the person's masters, teachers, guides, angels, and healing team to assist you. Begin the healing by hooking your third eye into the person's. Specifically imagine creating a beam of light in the form of a figure eight between your third eye and the person's; this creates a constant feedback loop for information between you.

The next step is to scan the person's aura and body in your imagination. Imagine that you have x-ray vision. Consciously use your third eye to scan. Imagine creating a laser beam of light - from your third eye, using it like a scope to examine the internal body. Scan the entire body with the mental probe, taking note of any energy blockages or negativity encountered. Trust the information you are being given. Take your time. The scanning process can take a long time in the beginning but, as you practice, the time spent becomes shorter and shorter.

Once you have determined what needs to be worked on, you can begin the actual healing. You can use any healing technique you would use for hands-on healing: pulling out negativity, channeling healing energy into the body, stimulating reflexology or acupuncture points, etc. Any technique you feel guided to use is fine. Use your creativity. Instead of physically performing the technique, imagine or visualize performing it. This includes imagining using toning or talking to the person. You can even be asking questions about where the person has pain. Some examples of creative ways to heal long distance are:

- Visualize using a rotor rooter to clear arteries or veins.
- Fill the cells or organs with light.
- If you see an area that needs draining, visualize inserting a faucet and using it to drain the area (you may sense a foul odor during this process).
- Use your hands as magnets to pull negativity out of the body (block your wrists energetically to protect yourself,) then shake the energy out physically or in your mind's eye.
- Invite a team of fairies to shovel out everything that is less than love.

- Psychically adjust the person's spine.
- Imagine swirling the chakras.
- Do whatever comes naturally.

The following are two additional techniques that also work well for absentee healing.

Use Positive Symbols to Place in the Person's Body. After you have finished doing the healing on the person, you can ask the soul to give you a positive symbol for perfect health for this person. Visualize this symbol on the tip of your third eye probe; use the probe to place the symbol inside the person's body at the base of the spine. Then wrap the symbol in colored layers of light, intuitively choosing which colors to use and in which order. Also fill the spine with white light. You can also place the symbol in their third eye instead, and do the color wrapping. I learned some of this material in the 1980's from a powerful healer named Moneca Taylor.

Create an Implant for Timed-release Healing. This is a variation on the symbol technique. The difference is that you will be programming the person's subconscious mind to activate the layers of colored light in order to release the healing energy over a period of time. The time of activation can vary from hours to weeks. This technique is especially good if you won't be available to work on the person in the future. I developed this technique when I was traveling to far-away places, such as India, for extended periods of time.

Begin this technique exactly like the symbol technique. Use the third eye probe to insert a symbol of perfect health in the person's body and layer it with light. The difference is that as you intuitively choose the layers of light, ask the person's soul when and for how long each layer is to be activated. Communicate this information to the person's subconscious mind and assign it the task of activating the various colors appropriately. The number of layer of color can vary from one to many; the time for activation of each color can vary from immediate to months away.

After you have completed the absentee healing, do one last scan to see if you missed anything. When you are complete, send deep love into the person, wrap the light of God around the person, and thank him/her for allowing you to do the work.

The absentee healing can also be done by groups as well. Years ago in the classes I was teaching, as a group we spiritually invited a person into the center of the group. Each person gave their impressions of what they were picking up as they scanned the individual. It was uncanny how many descriptions were alike. We then worked on the individual as a group. In some cases, we pre-arranged a situation where the target individual would be sitting or lying in a comfortable position, at the time we were to work on him/her. In these cases, we were able subsequently to get feedback from the people as to what they experienced. Many reported sensations and feelings of peace, power, pain reduction, clarity, and love.

All of the techniques for absentee healing also can be done with the person present in the room with you. In this case, you (or the group of healers) also visualize the scanning and healing rather than actually performing it physically. This technique is called psychic healing. In psychic healing, you involve the person by asking for feedback (e.g., Where is the pain? What are you feeling now? What colors do you feel we should use for timed-release healing?) It is exciting for the healer(s) and person receiving the healing to compare their experiences.

There are many, many forms of healing. Whether you are doing hands-on healing, psychic healing, or absentee healing, the number of possible techniques is as limitless as your creativity and imagination. Trust your intuition and enjoy!

FOUR

Past Lives

*P*ast lives is an exciting study. Edgar Cayce was one of the forerunners and teachers of our times who opened up this area of exploration and interest for us lightworkers. If you do believe you have lived before, this makes a regression session much easier. In fact, it is very easy to either regress yourself or someone else. After experimenting with different techniques, you easily can go to a past place in time just by moving into a relaxed and meditative state.

At some time in life, we become curious about past lives; this is when we may start having visions and flashbacks about previous incarnations. For instance, one that I saw recently occurred during a meditation. I suddenly became aware of the smell of smoke from a pipe. That sweet smell was so strong that I wondered where it was coming from and opened my eyes. Of course, I saw no one there and went back into meditation. The next thing I experienced was the smell of the sea. As I stayed with the experience, I was able to feel the mist from the waves coming over the bow of the ship I was standing on. At that point, it was clear to me that this vision felt very familiar. I decided to step back from the bow in my imagination to see an overview of the scene. When I did, I was able to see a sea captain standing there with gray hair and wearing a "P" coat. His hat was pulled down on his head. He was a big man and he loved the sea. I actually could smell his skin and feel his gentle ruggedness. Suddenly it was clear to me that this man was me. I was able to identify the essence in him and it was the same essence, or soul, as mine.

There are many schools of thought about how many lives we live on Earth. Some say three, some say a few, but my feeling is that our lives number in the thousands. If, indeed, Earth has been inhabited for millions of years, and we all would like to believe that we are "old souls," it stands to reason that we've been around the block a few thousand times. There are probably millions of previous lifetimes elsewhere. We also live parallel lives in other universes and have many extensions of the soul. We left God billions of years ago and are now beginning our ascent back again. In the Mystery School where I studied sixteen years ago, it was said that it could well be that our last five hundred life times alone were the lives that we are currently working with to release the old victim behaviors we have accrued over the years.

Some of us wonder why we aren't all able to see our past lives. The explanation that makes sense to me is that a veil is placed between us and the majority of our consciousness. Depak Chopra says we have access only to a very limited amount of our mind. Why is this so? Because we are HUGH and, if we were able to experience everything that is in our mind, including all the lifetimes we've had, it would be a little overwhelming, don't you agree?

Everything I've read and brought through my channel indicates that we are able to experience the Big Picture from the soul and spirit levels, but we are veiled when we come down into a body. Some believe we were veiled by another species and that all of our DNA strands were cut except for two. We forget who we are again and again - until we awaken consciously. I think we are in the Big Awakening now, right here and now in this time and this place - Earth - and it is so very exciting!

DEMONSTRATION OF A PAST-LIFE REGRESSION

There are many different techniques for doing a regression. I will give two examples for you to use to start practicing. Soon you will develop your own technique as your soul begins to bring in methods from your past incarnations. You DO have your own style and this stands true in all respects and areas.

Have the person either sit or lie in a comfortable position, in a quiet place that is safe. Ask what the person wishes to see and learn (e.g., past incarnations with family members, the source of phobias). You want to establish a goal so you aren't just wandering around hoping to find something or someone of interest.

Also, begin the regression with the intention of healing the past traumas if there are any. Some lifetimes have no trauma or emotional charge; they are revealed to provide information.

Have the person close his/her eyes and take some deep breaths to relax and slow down the nervous system. Instruct the person to trust the first thought, feeling, or impression and not to doubt what he/she is getting. Also inform the person that the voice heard (if that happens) very well may be his/her own and that much of what is seen or felt may seem familiar. Tell the person to trust it all. The experience can be talked about later. Also there can be two lifetimes overlapping and the scenario may get confusing. Keep the person on track and speak in a calm, soothing voice.

Exercise One

Say the following to the person. Remember, you want to have the person sensually involved. (Instructions and explanatory notes in parentheses.)

Imagine that you are standing in a beautiful forest. The sun is shining warmly and you can feel the heat on your body. Walk through the forest on a path. I will be walking behind you to keep you company. Soon you will come to a stream and hear the sounds of water. Imagine how fresh and cool it is. There is a very large tree a few feet from the stream. Stand in front of the tree and feel its strength and safety.

Now walk over to the water and notice that there is a leaf flowing down the stream. Reach out and get the leaf. Make yourself tiny and lie on the leaf. Start paddling up the stream, feeling the cold water on your arms and legs, and the warmth of the sun on your body. Continue paddling up the stream. As you do, you are going backward in time. Notice the beautiful blades of grass with dew on them. As you paddle further up the stream, you are moving backward, backward in time. Notice the wild roses and their aroma on the left bank.

As you continue to paddle up the stream and further back in time, you soon find yourself going under a bridge. Feel the coolness of the shade on your body. As you come out the other side of the bridge, look back and notice that there are flowers growing over the bridge.

Soon you come to a very thick mist. Paddle through it, continuing backward in time. When you come out the other side, you notice that you are in a very large body of water. We are looking for a particular lifetime where you will find (state reason for the regression). One of the shores, where you find this lifetime, beckons to you. Tell me which shore you travel along to find this particular experience, the right shore or the left. Go to that shore and paddle along it, going backward, backward in time.

As you move along the shore, a place along it soon beckons to you. Continue paddling backward in time until you reach the place where you find (restate reason for the regression). (If it seems the person is taking a long time finding this place, nudge him/her along by asking, "Are you there yet?")

Once you reach the shore, get off the leaf, pull it up onto the shore, and make yourself large again. Now, walk up the bank to the crest and tell me what you see. You may see a village, city, or countryside. (Have the person describe the place. If he/she is having trouble seeing, tell him/her to imagine the landscape.)

Now, walk toward (name the place). (If the person doesn't see anything, have him/her start walking until someone or something appears.)

As soon as you arrive in (name of place), go to the center of the village, town or area and stand there until a building or particular area beckons to you. Go to it. Look around and describe what you see. (Ask questions appropriate to determining where the person is, who is with him/her, and what is happening. Have the person describe anyone who seems significant and ask what is the relationship to that person [father, son, employer]. Also ask if the person knows any of the participants now, in the current lifetime. Have the person describe the scenario, what is happening.)

Past-life memories usually involve some sort of painful event or trauma. Let the person experience it. It is important for him/her to feel the emotion of it. Once the experience is over, it is time to heal the memory. This is important because it heals present-time relationships.

To heal the memory, have the person go back to the traumatic episode/abuse and use your creativity to redo the scene in a positive way. The subconscious mind is not able to differentiate between the past and present; when it views a healing happening in the past, it assumes that situation is happening in present time.

If the person was a victim, have him/her defend his/her self. The person may have to get violent to even the score and balance the karma. If the person was a perpetrator, have the event never happen, or have the perpetrator become loving, or allow the victim to successfully defend him or herself. Revise the scenario so there is forgiveness on both parts. There must be a healing of the memory. If the person gets stuck emotionally and can't forgive or get even, have him/her do the best possible. Tell the person that he/she may work out the anger, fear, or hurt in the dream state. Or the person may need to be regressed again at a later time.

After this healing, the other person(s) involved at some level also will experience something. And the person will be changed because there is balance now in that relationship. It is very easy to heal wounds using past-life regression.

Before you bring the person out of the past lifetime, ask the location, the year or time period, and his/her name then. If the person doesn't know, move on quickly; you don't want to get the person's mind engaged too much, and you don't want the person to doubt the process.

Have the person thank all people involved in the memory "scene" and return to the large body of water. Reverse the regression technique to bring him/her back to present time. (Remember, the mist may not be there; it represents the veil.)

Find your leaf, make yourself small again, and paddle back into the water. Paddle back across the water, through the mist, and to the stream. As you go you are paddling forward in time. Enter the stream and begin floating down the stream, moving forward in time. You are passing the bridge, the roses, and the blades of grass covered with dew. The water is cool and the sun is warm on your body as you come forward to the present time (you can state the current year).

Come back to the place where the tree is standing in the forest. Paddle over to the bank, get off the leaf, release it to the stream, and stand under the tree. Return to full size. Now come back to this room and to the chair. Move your hands and feet. (This grounds the person into the body in present time.)

Now discuss what happened: What the person experienced and how it relates to resolving the issue identified as the purpose for the regression. If you feel this person needs more work on this memory, because it may be deep-seated or impacted and is a theme pattern (habit), it is wise to suggest that the person allow you to help him/her further in another session. Also be available to this person by phone if you feel he/he could drop into depression.

You have done a great service in helping this person clear the past; now the memories will leave the body. Advise the person to drink a lot of water to remove any toxins or residue from the physical body.

Exercise Two

Now that you have the idea about how regression is done, it will be easy to follow another exercise or create your own.

I usually look at the person's personality type. Is this person spacey or grounded? This sometimes determines which method to use. For a spacey person, it is helpful to use a visualization that takes him/her underground (e.g., into a cave or into the side of a mountain). For a very grounded person, it is easier for the person to experience in an elevated situation (e.g., hop on a flying carpet or take an elevator). If you are not sure, ask if the person is predominantly spacey or grounded. Here is an example that works well for spacey people. (Remember to get the senses involved).

Let us take a journey back in time. We'll walk through a forest to an opening in a mountainside that has moss growing over it. Go inside and light a candle or lantern. Take a look around and describe the surroundings. Begin walking through this cave and, as you go, you are moving backward in time. (If you feel this person needs to go deeper into a near-hypnotic state, you can actually count down as you have the person climb down a ladder or steps that take him/her further back into the past.)

The walls of the cave are damp and the air is cool. You can hear water dripping. As you walk, you are going further and further backward in time.

Soon you come to a fork in the cave. One fork leads to the lifetime where (state purpose of regression). Which fork is it? Walk down this fork. As you continue backward in time, you come to a place where you see a light or an opening in the roof of the cave. This opening will lead you to the lifetime we are seeking. (When the person reaches this opening, have him/her climb a ladder; when he/she gets to the top, have the person describe what is seen.)

From this point on, follow the same guidelines given in the previous exercise. Have the person find the place, describe the setting, identify the people involved, and experience the event. Then use your creativity to revise the situation to heal the memory.

This has been a brief introduction to the subject of

past lives, but it is enough to get you started. If you would like more information, one of my friends and clients who studied with me for years is writing a comprehensive book on this subject. Jean Rita Linder helped me write this book. *Her book, The Past Lives: Using Past Lives as a Tool for Transformation and Growth*, demonstrates how exploring our past lives can help us expand our consciousness, heal wounds, and foster emotional and spiritual growth. It includes more than a dozen full regressions that she and I did during her sessions with me.

FIVE

Mind-Clearing Techniques

MEDITATION

*M*editation takes many forms and can be done in any setting - sitting quietly in a dark room, walking, dancing, performing marshal arts, or sitting on a bus. It can take place at any time of the day or night, with eyes opened or closed. A basic definition of meditation is that when you meditate, you still the mind and connect with the inner godself.

I have been a disciplined meditator for many years. The results I have received are a sense of oneness with God, a quiet mind (most of the time), the ability to make wise decisions and actions as a natural and automatic function, a slowing down and distressing of the brain and nervous system, and a reduction of anxiety and fear.

At some point, usually after many years of disciplined regular meditation, you can reach the most wonderful state of bliss! The mind becomes incredibly quiet; there is no awareness of any outside interference, there is only stillness inside. Sometimes high states are reached and there is nothing but blue light and union with All That Is. These precious moments make a huge difference in the nervous system. Quantum healing and a cessation of the aging process can happen. Stress lines disappear from the body. A calmness is felt. There is nothing more satisfying and peaceful than this experience of the Divine. The Sanskrit word for this state is *samadi*.

New meditators experience two things: (1) They have difficulty stilling the mind. (2) They expect *samadi* the first time and are disappointed, discouraged, and ready to give it all up after fifteen minutes. They assume they are just not any good at meditation.

Meditation needs to be approached from a very basic position. Begin by teaching yourself to sit in the same place, at the same time, every day for at least twenty minutes - even if your mind chatters the entire time. Choose a place where you will not be interrupted. Be firm in setting your boundaries with others.

There are several different techniques for getting into a meditative state. One technique is to sit in a dark room and gaze at the flame of a candle for about five minutes, allowing any negative thoughts to leave. Become single-pointed in your focus. As soon as your mind has become reasonably still, blow out the candle and sit with your back erect. Your hands can be placed palms up or down on your lap. Take deep breaths to release all tension from your body. Breathe in light and love and exhale all stress. Sit for fifteen minutes more.

A second technique is using breath work. Take slow breaths in and out; with each breath you drop deeper and deeper inside. If the chatter starts in your mind, gently whisper, "No." Each time a thought comes up, whisper, "No." Soon, you will teach yourself to ignore the chatter:

the laundry list, the things you have to do tomorrow, how your daughter is doing, how you performed at work today, whatever. The mind is in the habit of rerunning all these thoughts - all these tapes; so you must teach it to be quiet for at least twenty minutes each day. As soon as your mind has gotten quiet, you can stop the conscious breathing and go back to your normal breathing and settle in.

A third technique is to sit erect with your hands in your lap or on your knees, palms up or palms down. Take deep breaths in and out, releasing the tensions and concerns of the day and bringing in light and love. Become conscious of your chakra system. The second chakra is in the middle of the belly. Imagine that you are standing facing yourself, and imagine that the second chakra is like a clock. With the flat of your hand, begin to swirl the second chakra in a clockwise manner. The circle gets bigger and bigger until you feel the chakra swirling on its own. Then begin chanting "OM" while the chakra swirls on its own. After chanting for a few minutes, do the Pranayama Breathwork Technique described below, in the section "Pattern Removal." This time when you hold your breath, after twenty breaths squeeze the sphincter muscle (the one that stops the flow of urine). When you release your breath, release the muscle. Do this breathing technique four or five times. Then sit back and relax. Your mind should be very clear and quiet by now. Enjoy the silence as you drop deeper inside.

Twenty minutes of meditation often has substituted for hours of sleep for some people because all the body systems slow down and have the opportunity to regenerate. All people benefit from meditation and if you can only sit for a few minutes a day, that is a good start. You will sit in the same place each time for meditating, and the reason is to build a "power spot." Only you should sit there. Your "inner meditator" will call you in at the same time each day after you have been practicing for a while. So, plan on "being there" to answer the call. You are forming a new habit.

PATTERN REMOVAL

Within the subconscious mind are millions of beliefs. Some are positive, some are not. If you have an understanding of how the subconscious mind works, it makes it easier to aid in the process of eliminating your nonpositive beliefs. The subconscious mind is like a computer. It does not have the discernment to understand what is appropriate and what is not. It has been programmed from our past experiences, both from this life and past lives. As a computer, it cannot discern what beliefs should stay and what should be eliminated. It does not know what is healthy and life-supporting and what is not. Here is an example of how these beliefs are established in the subconscious mind:

In your first experience on planet Earth, your emotional and mental bodies were pure except for theme issues. You had no preconceptions about what life on Earth would be like. Let's say you are walking on a beach and decide to walk into this liquid form that is water, the ocean. Your first perception is that it feels pure and cool and refreshing. So, you decide to move your body out deeper into the ocean, perhaps swimming or floating. So your beliefs about what ocean is, are positive. Then suppose a huge wave submerges you and you almost drown. Whether you die or not, your new belief is, "Ocean is dangerous." You then begin to avoid this dangerous place, or maybe the subconscious mind creates a fear of drowning. So, this beautiful, refreshing body of liquid suddenly has become dangerous.

Then you venture into a forest, hearing the birds chirping, feeling the warm sun shining down on you. You feel safe and comforted. This is your first impression of forest. Suddenly a bear comes from behind a tree and attacks you. Whether you die or not, the positive belief is now replaced with the negative memory of the bear attack. Forest is now dangerous.

Distorted beliefs are compounded within the mind and emotions. As soon as the emotional body forms an impression, positive or not, the mind picks up that feeling and turns it into a thought, and our reality changes. We are leery of "dangerous" places because our survival has been challenged.

When many false beliefs come together, they create a form called a "pattern," and it is multi-layered like an onion. Ultimately, after thousands of lifetimes on Earth, we have created many phobias and patterns of false beliefs within ourselves due to the massive amount of distorted information. Many times, we do not even know where these phobias or negative beliefs come from, because they have been reinforced over thousands of lifetimes and subconsciously have become our truth. These false beliefs are now our subconscious belief system.

The ego/mental body's job is to protect us. So, for obvious reasons, you hear a warning to avoid dangerous people, places, and things. Sometimes, due to the distortions in the subconscious mind, these dangerous things can include success, love, happiness, and/or abundance. Obviously, these are the things we all want. So, the question becomes: How do we break down the old belief system, so we can have a full, passionate life without living in constant fear of being killed, abandoned, or hurt?

CLEARING PATTERNS

By using different visualizations, you can clear away these nonpositive patterns by removing one layer at a time from the "onion" of compounded false beliefs. To get to the core of the onion, you may find many times that other aspects or parts of your belief system are intertwined. So, once you have cleared the top layer, you may find yourself having memories of an entirely different area or issue. For instance, you may be clearing issues about financial sustenance, and your parents' thoughts may surface which tie financial abundance in with self-worth (e.g., "I'm not good enough to deserve wealth," "I have to work hard for money," "No pain, no gain," "Men deserve more money than women," etc. So, now you have more areas to be cleared: self-worth, separation of genders, and on and on.

After many years of clearing myself, my style of helping others now is to take the first layer off the top, all the way across the top, including all other areas that may be connected. When working with a person in an hour session, I ask the person for two main issues to clear. Then the unwinding begins. The unwinding creates space in the auric field and between the cells where new, positive input can be infused. Then, after the person has integrated the new positive suggestions and light, a second session can be used to remove the next layer. Therefore, over time, a new more positive belief system is created and awareness begins to change. Eventually, peace, happiness, faith, trust, love, and all the higher energy feelings and thoughts become part of the person's reality.

PATTERN REMOVAL TECHNIQUES

By using different techniques, we remove the old and replace it with the new. There are many techniques that can be used, probably thousands. For example, Dr. Bernie Seagal has his cancer patients communicate with the disease to find out what the disease wants, why it is here, what feelings created it. As soon as the patient replaces the old beliefs with new, positive ones, forgiveness can happen within the patient and the cancer begins to dissolve. People call this a miracle. To me, being in the right place at the right time is a miracle. When our mind is clear, we are in sync with the universe and miracles are waiting for us.

Rapid Eye Movement. A very simple technique for clearing nonpositive beliefs is rapid eye movement. This one can be done on yourself, or you can facilitate someone else. Close your eyes. Drop your consciousness inside your being. Ask what the feeling is that is causing your frustration or blocked energy. Ask for one word such as fear, hopelessness, anger, or loneliness. (Note: If the word you get identifies a thought or issue, as opposed to a feeling, you are on the mental level of the conscious mind rather than the emotional level or subconscious mind. It may be necessary to clear this level first, because the feeling may be masked by thoughts. The short cut is to go straight in and identify the underlying feeling.)

As soon as you have the word, open your eyes. Cross your forefinger and middle finger on one hand, as you would to symbolize good luck. Begin saying the word out loud and move the hand with the crossed fingers horizontally back and forth at eye level. Hold your head still and follow the moving hand with your eyes twenty times, continuing to say the word out loud. You should feel a release. Know that the release process could continue for days after you do the exercise. Always drink a lot of water and breath deeply to aid your clearing process. It really is a process.

Pranayama Breathwork Technique. Pranayama is a Sanskrit word for chi, meaning life force. Deep breathing activates this life force in the subtle bodies. In addition, when you hold your breath in the body, you stimulate the kundalini energy. Therefore, this technique is using the breath to stimulate energy and clear negativity. This technique begins in the same way as the Rapid Eye Movement technique. Close your eyes and go inside and ask for a word that identifies the underlying feeling. Think about the feeling and feel it in your body. Make it real in present time. Imagine that it is activated right now. This exercise works on the mental, emotional, and physical levels, so it is important to think about and feel the emotion throughout the exercise to engage all three bodies.

With your eyes closed, take twenty breaths, in and out through the nose. Use your solar plexus as a pump. You can even put your hand on your solar plexus to feel the pumping action as you breath in and out through the nose. Your breathing should be slow and steady. I have found that rapid breathing clears the higher chakras, while slow breathing clears the lower chakras. Emotional issues reside in the three lower chakras. Hold the twentieth breath as long as you can, then release it. Now do twenty more breaths, continuing to think about and feel the emotion as you breathe. Do a total of four twenty-breath sequences. Then relax and contemplate the new awareness or resolution that has replaced the old program and associated feelings. You can then wait a few days, then check back inside yourself. You will find that the old issue has dissipated and the next layer is ready to be exposed. Repeat this exercise of four twenty-breath sequences on the new word/emotion.

Dvorak Breathwork Technique. I learned this technique from Jim Dvorak in the 1980s. It is very simple and effective for clearing negative energy from the body and aura. Close your eyes and go inside and ask for an issue that needs to be cleared. After you identify the issue, continue to think about it. Now, with your eyes closed, turn your head to the right (as if you are going to look over your right shoulder) and say out loud, "I am willing to release this pattern." Then breathe in and simultaneously turn your head from the right to the left. (In this movement, you start with your head looking over your right shoulder, then turn it 180 degrees to look over your left shoulder.) After your head has been turned all the way to the left, pause; then release your breath as you turn your head back to face forward. Now take four short, fast breaths in and out; then one long, slow, deep breath in and out. This technique can be used by itself or after any other clearing technique to clean any residual debris or negative energy from all the bodies, physical and subtle.

Tornado Technique. This technique came from the Tibetan Foundation. It was channeled from the Master Djwhal Kuhl through Janet McClure, the founder. It can be used daily as a quick energizing and clearing method. Imagine that you are standing in a glass tube, twelve feet in diameter, extending from the earth up into the spiritual plane. Imagine seeing words being written, printed, or typed at your feet in darkness. There will be a statement or "title" that explains what you want to clear. Then, ask your subconscious mind to tell you all the reasons why you can't do this. These will appear printed below the title. Following are two examples of a title and limiting beliefs from the subconscious as you might see them written, typed or printed at your feet in darkness:

REMOVING ALL MY FEAR It is too late. It is hopeless. No way to get through the fears. There are too many. Not good enough. Not powerful enough. Stuck.

MOVING BEYOND LIMITATION Stuck here. Fear of losing my identity. Can't see the other side. Too risky.

Once you visualize the words, imagine a huge golden tornado coming down through the tube, sweeping around your body, sucking all the words up from around your feet, taking all the negative energy out the top of the tube, including any negative energy that may be pulled from all your bodies. Visualize all of this being sucked out the top of the tube into the spiritual plane where angels transmute the energy and send it back to the earth as love.

After all the nonpositive energy has been sucked out the top, imagine looking back down around your feet and seeing light and the words, joy and love bouncing up and down. You have removed the darkness and nonpositive thoughts and feelings and have replaced them with positive images of light, love, and joy.

You can follow this tornado technique with the Dvorak Breathwork Technique for additional clearing.

SYMBOLOGY

I learned this technique from a good friend, Victor Mull. The subconscious mind works in symbols and pictures. Learning the language of symbols is like learning another language. If you ask the mind to give you the answer to a question, you may be shown a picture or have a certain feeling in a particular part of your body, like a pain or pressure. Deciphering the messages from your subconscious is an exciting realization process because you are being given a map. This map tells you where you have been and where you are going, much like dreams.

When you break down the dream or symbols from the subconscious mind, you are able to understand what they represent, and then can work with the issues. Use the symbol as a focal point, asking what it means and/or what it represents. It will take you on a journey and give you the answer you are looking for. Sometimes the symbol will be a memory; this is called an association. The question you have asked the mind will be associated with something that happened in the past. Sometimes you may get a flashback of yourself in a past life. The purpose of the process is to get deeper and deeper into the subconscious and learn what your symbols are so it becomes easier to understand what is going on in your life.

In using symbology as a clearing technique, you can use it either on yourself or to facilitate another. The person sits down and closes his/her eyes. Have the person identify an issue or block that he/she wants to clear. Then ask the person to ask his/her subconscious mind to give you a symbol or picture to represent this issue. The person may see a picture or symbol, hear a word, imagine an incident, feel pressure or pain in the body; or the subconscious may show a number of different symbols. The first impression is always the correct clue and the one you should work with.

If the person does not see anything, ask what he/she feels or what was the first thought. Sometimes people get into perfectionism and expect a dramatic, undeniable answer; this overcomplicates the technique.

This is very subtle work and it is important to identify the first impression, no matter how fleeting or "imperfect" it may seem to be. The person also may invalidate his/her own inner voice, so always emphasize reporting the first impression, no matter what form it takes.

Whatever symbol the person identifies, it is not your role to interpret it. Instead, ask the person to ask the subconscious what the symbol means. For example, if the person identifies a triangle, that symbol does have a universal meaning, the trinity. However, to the person it may mean something entirely different; for example, a three-sided relationship. All symbols are individual in meaning. Each subconscious has its own unique language.

After the subconscious has indicated the meaning of the symbol, ask the person how this meaning relates to the issue to be cleared. Again, it is not your role as facilitator to draw conclusions. The person must do his/her own work, because this is an essential part of the realization process.

The person becomes empowered by identifying the answers him or herself. If the person comes up with a symbol and really cannot break it down or analyze it, you may need to guide him/her to the answer by asking related questions. Once you understand the process, it becomes very simple and fun.

Once the meaning of the symbol has been connected to the issue, and the person consciously understands it, then ask the person either to wrap the symbol in the light of God, or burn it with fire until it dissolves. Most of the time, the symbol will dissolve. If any part remains, have the person ask the subconscious mind what that remaining part means. As soon as the person has an understanding of this, he/she can wrap the light of God around the remaining part, or burn it. If the symbol will not dissolve, it may be necessary to use one of the breathwork techniques described in the "Pattern Removal" section. After the person has done the breath work, try again to burn the remaining portion, or wrap the light of God around it. Sometimes the ego just does not want to let go of a belief, pattern or habit.

On rare occasions, the ego can be so resistant that it may be important to dialog with the ego. Have the person ask the ego to stand before him/her. Have the person ask the ego what it is afraid of losing. Control is the usual issue. At this point, it is important to enlist the help of the ego; give it a job to do to assist the clearing process. For example, ask the ego to be the one to burn the remaining piece of the symbol. Now that you have given the ego a sense of participation (control), things usually will go much smoother and the symbol should easily transmute.

Now ask the person to ask the subconscious mind for another symbol that represents the original issue. Then go through the process again with this symbol: identifying what it means, how it relates to the issue, and finally dissolving it in light or fire. Enlist the aid of the ego if necessary.

Continue this process of identifying symbols until there are no more. It usually takes an average of three symbols to get to the core of an issue. During the process, the person will be making a lot of realizations about him or herself. In the days following the application of the symbology technique, as the changes integrate, additional information may surface and more realizations probably will be made. Conclude this process, and all other clearing techniques, by having the person thank all parts of him or herself for participation and help. Ask the person to keep a daily journal to see the progress.

INNER CHILD

Discovering Your Inner Child

I first discovered my inner child when I was doing some inner exploration. I was trying to find out who was in my body. In response to my question, "Who is inside of me?" I was shown a little girl hiding under a chair in a very dark corner of the room. I imagined getting down on my hands and knees and looking under the chair. She was very ragged. She looked like a little orphan. Her face was very dirty. She was wearing a torn dress. She was terrified and lashed out at me like a little animal. I kept trying to get her to come out from underneath the chair and she would not. Getting her to trust me was very difficult; it took several attempts. I finally succeeded by telling her I'd give her love. When she finally came out, she looked awful. I imagined taking her outside to a creek and bathing her. I shampooed and brushed her hair. She looked bruised and battered. I visualized putting another little dress on her. I held her and kissed her. She was terribly frightened, and she was very angry with me and with everybody.

You never know what you are going to get when you begin to meet different parts of yourself. One day you can pull out a healthy child or adolescent; the next time a real traumatized child emerges. Over time, you get to know all different aspects of yourself.

Throughout our lives, we experience different traumas. Often we become emotionally "stuck" at the age of the child who experienced the trauma. We can become the typical "person who never grows up." Or we can revert to that age when we experience a similar trauma. The association flips us back to that young age emotionally, and we react and respond in present time as we did as a child. It is important, at any age, to heal these wounded parts of ourselves, to allow us to "grow up" and become a mature, healthy adult.

Nurturing the Inner Child to Learn Self-Love

A lot is resolved though inner child work. We visualize loving our inner child. That precious little being is us. When we give love to our inner child, wonderful things begin to happen. We begin to understand that we are our own source of love. Perhaps our parents did not love us in the way we needed to be loved. Maybe they did not know how because their parents did not demonstrate love to them. Whatever the patterns have been from generation to generation, there usually is a needy child within us who needs our love. Once we learn how to love ourself, we become self-sustaining. We become one with our own godself. We become whole. This is an essential prelude to becoming enlightened. As long as we continue to search for love outside of self, we are not healing ourself and we cannot become whole. We remain needy and dependent on others. In fact, we have everything inside that we need to sustain us. This is what inner child work helps us to discover.

ACCESSING AND NURTURING YOUR INNER CHILD

This is a very simple exercise. It can be done on yourself, or you can facilitate others. Begin by having the person close his/her eyes and ask for the inner child to appear in the mind's eye. If the person can't see the inner child, have him/her feel or imagine its presence. Have the person ask the inner child to sit on his/her lap. Have the person look at the inner child or get an impression of what this child looks like. If the person can't see, then have him/her imagine what the inner child looks like. How old is the child? Is it male or female? (We each have both male and female inner parts of self.) What is the child's name? It may or may not be the same name as the person.

Have the person talk with the child to establish a trusting relationship. Then the nurturing process begins. Find out what the child would like to have or do. Have the person imagine giving the child whatever it wants. It may be a trip to the park or the zoo. Flying a kite. Eating ice cream cones together. Have the person re-parent the inner child by becoming the new healthy, loving, attentive mommy or daddy. Whatever the inner child wants, give it to him/her. Usually the child wants whatever the person didn't get when he/she was a child. If you deny/denied yourself sugar, your child may want the forbidden sugar. Give it to him/her. Imagine acting out a whole scenario between the child and the new mommy or daddy. Whatever comes up, allow it. Whatever the interaction is between the person and the inner child, be very loving and supportive of both.

This is usually a very emotional experience. Don't be surprised if the person experiences a very deep sadness. Tears are almost inevitable and this is very healing. These little inner children need to express emotion. They may have been taught to hide their feelings and may have trained themselves not to cry or show emotion, for fear of punishment or rejection. Explain to the person that this is a safe place and encourage him/her to cry or get angry. Let the person feel whatever needs to be felt. Sometimes, as a defense mechanism, a person on the verge of tears instead will begin to laugh. Discourage this. Encourage the person instead to go deeper and feel whatever emotion is buried inside, needing to be expressed. Two things will be learned by this. (1) It is safe to cry; it will not kill you. (2) It is incredibly healing to honor your feelings.

It is important for you, the facilitator, not to become too emotionally involved in this process. It is critical for you to stay very grounded (see "Grounding," chapter three). If you lose control and become emotional, you are no longer able to help your clients or friends with their healing processes.

This process of meeting and nurturing one's inner child is really just a beginning. It is an ongoing process of paying attention to and loving the child in you. One helpful exercise is to buy a doll that looks like and represents the inner child. You can sleep with the doll, talk with it, play with it, whatever feels good to you. This doll is a surrogate.

Getting Answers From the Inner Child

Inner Child work is one of the best ways to identify inner truths and unresolved issues. Many people are not at all in touch with their needs or who they are. This process is a very easy way to address these problems. The inner child becomes the third party and the one who knows and can reveal the secrets. Your inner child almost always will give you an answer. You can employ this "inner voice" to help you heal.

For example, I have a friend, Don Sambol, who was not able to visualize anything psychically. We found a way around that. I was asking him to see something. He said, "You know I can't see anything. That is not one of my gifts." I said, "Ask your little boy what he sees. "Oh, well, he sees..."

If a person can't see, have the inner child see for him/her. The inner child often can see what you, the adult, cannot. And you usually get a straight answer from the inner child.

There is a child in every chakra, and each chakra performs a different purpose. For example, the third eye sees and the throat chakra expresses. But the child in each chakra is not limited to those issues and can give you information about what the other chakras are holding. If one child does not know an answer, you can call on another. You can go into multiple chakras and pull out multiple children until you get an answer. If you ask them about thoughts or feelings, you may come up with different answers. You may want to bring out two chakra children and ask them the same question to find out if there is a conflict within. The heart child may be excited about doing something, but the second or third chakra child may not be at all interested. You can find out what different parts of yourself are up to. And you can use these children to help identify and resolve the issues within. Some chakras are mental and some are emotional. It is really exciting to work with these children.

MASCULINE-FEMININE BALANCE

Freud and Jung talked about the masculine-feminine aspects of self from a psychological perspective. It is an essential part of who we are as human beings. It is very important to balance the masculine and feminine energies within. This is essential in the enlightenment process. It is usually one of the last pieces of the puzzle in the evolutionary plan.

Within each of us there is a masculine essence and a feminine essence. The masculine aspect or part of self is in the right side of the body; the feminine aspect is in the left side. This corresponds to the right and left hemispheres of the brain which cross over and control opposite sides of the body. The right brain, which controls the left side of the body, is intuitive, passive, and creative. The left brain is logical, practical, and forceful, and it controls the right side of the body. The left side of the brain is the mental; the right side is the emotional.

The masculine aspect of self is aggressive, dynamic, and light like a sun blazing forth. The light of the masculine represents the active energy that thrusts us forward. The masculine energy is the doer. The feminine aspect of self is intuitive, creative, passive, and dark like the moon. The darkness of the feminine represents the creative force, the womb. From the darkness comes the light. The darkness gives birth to the light. This is why, through time, women have been referenced as the dark sex. Women powerfully and silently sit back and empower others through the creativeness of the feminine aspect. The feminine also is the healer within. If someone is going to be a healer, the feminine force must come through. The masculine energy

- not to be confused with the male - is not capable of healing. All it can do is to get the healer to settle down and rest for a while so he/she can be a conduit and allow the healing force to flow. If the healer is a male, he must allow his feminine aspect to heal through him.

There are many ramifications when the masculine and feminine aspects are out of balance. When somebody has accidents, or bangs into walls, or starts dropping things, sometimes that can be caused by masculine-feminine imbalance. If you can get the person's masculine and feminine into alignment, chances are his/her overall sense of balance will return and the accidents will stop.

Also, masculine-feminine imbalance is the key to most relationship problems. When there is a battle going on within due to an imbalance, this is usually reflected in external relationships. Masculine-feminine imbalance leads to power struggles with other people. It involves the second chakra that is the center of our power. If there is an imbalance in this area, there is probably a power struggle going on within the person. If the masculine and feminine parts of self are prejudiced against each other, and/or are fighting or rebelling against each other, and/or are fighting for control, what happens outwardly? The same thing. We fight with everyone around us. We are constantly in competition. If we are not balanced within, our power becomes misguided and misdirected.

This is also a separation issue. When the inner male and female are not in balance, they are separate from each other. This also separates us from God. By bringing the masculine and feminine together, they love each other and become one. As a result, we feel good and our bodies are healthy and balanced. We love ourselves and all humankind.

When you are dealing with masculine-feminine balance, it doesn't matter what gender or sexual preference you are. Both men and women have masculine and feminine aspects. And it does not matter if you are homosexual or heterosexual. If there is a distortion within the masculine-feminine balance, whoever or whatever you are will be distorted. Conversely, if you are balanced, you can have beautiful relationships. It is all the same. And it is all one. It is all a piece of God.

Part of the process of balancing the masculine and feminine aspects is determining all the old, negative beliefs and patterns about men and women and relationships that were handed down to us by our parents. Unfortunately, until we identify and clear these issues, inevitably we choose a mate with the most undesirable characteristics and behavior of both parents. We choose such a mate because he/she mirrors back to us the issues we need to resolve.

Many spiritual people stay single for years because they are afraid to work on this issue. They are afraid of being hurt and/or rejected again as they were in past relationships. Balancing the polarity aspect of self is a painful process, but essential. Unfortunately, the best way to work through these issues is through relationships. That is the purpose of relationships. We learn by experiencing and observing ourselves in relationship to others.

The balancing process begins by identifying the inherited negative beliefs and patterns that simply aren't working anymore. Once we identify and partially clear these self-destructive behaviors, the search can begin for a healthy partner. Now we think we have it all together. We have read all the self-help books. We have taken all the workshops. We've done years of therapy. We have our list of desired characteristics for our mate. We are convinced we can "walk the talk" and magically find Mr./Ms. Right.

Wrong! This is where the real work begins.

Usually we get an opportunity to experience and practice all that we have learned. We get to practice and integrate these new concepts up close and personal in a new relationship, or a series of relationships. We magnetically pull to ourselves our equal, and the perfect person with whom to practice. As soon as the "honeymoon/puppy love" phase is over and all the great sex has been had, this wonderful person drops the sheep's cloak to reveal Mommy/Daddy Wolf with big, hurtful teeth. But don't despair. Remember, these are your practice relationships.

It is then time to go back to the drawing board for deeper self-examination. Ask yourself, what went wrong? Nothing. This was practice. Since you have never had a healthy relationship, and probably have never even seen one, you continue to act out the old habits and behaviors, only this time with a conscious awareness of what you are experiencing. You are learning through doing. However, if you are able to create a healthy relationship in the first attempt, my hat is off to you.

Now the list of ideal characteristics for a healthy mate gets reworked. The lessons have been learned on a deeper experiential level. Now you really "get it." You can finally magnetically draw in an equal who is ready to learn with you how to have a healthy relationship. Now you are ready to complete masculine-feminine balance in yourself.

At any point in the process, it is helpful to go inside and examine your own inner masculine/feminine aspects to see how healthy this internal relationship is, because any internal imbalances are reflected externally in relationships. The bottom line with balancing the masculine and feminine within is that we become whole. We become whole emotionally, mentally, and spiritually.

An Exercise to Balance Masculine and Feminine

In this exercise, you establish a dialog between the masculine and feminine parts of yourself to find out what they do and do not like about each other. If you can get the masculine and feminine to talk to each other, and find out what their differences are, you then usually can come to some sort of an understanding between the two. The dialog hopefully moves them into a relationship based on mutual respect and support. Ideally this leads to peace between them so they can come together in a beautiful dance, a love affair. If the masculine and feminine parts of self can love each other, what will happen is you automatically will begin to balance and come into alignment within yourself.

I frequently talk with my masculine and feminine aspects. If I find myself making nasty remarks about men or if I experience conflicts with the people in my life, I ask my inner male and female to come out and I visualize them standing before me. I ask the female, "What does the male look like to you? What is it about him that you are angry with?" And I ask the male the same questions about the female. All the problems in life are about something going on within. It has nothing to do with anyone else. One time I heard myself say, "All men are dogs." I wondered where that came from, so I went inside and asked my feminine aspect why she thinks all men are dogs. And she said, "Because my dad was." So, then I knew the source of the false belief. What I did was to get the masculine and feminine together and have her see that her mate, my inner masculine, was not a dog. I helped her identify his wonderful qualities. Once those two talked, she wasn't angry anymore.

I will describe the exercise as if you are facilitating for someone. You can also do this exercise on yourself. Have the person ask the masculine aspect of self to come out of the right side of the pelvic area (this is the relationship chakra) and stand before the person. Ask the person to describe what the masculine aspect looks like. (If the person does not see him, have the person imagine what the masculine aspect looks like or feel what he looks like.) Find out how old the aspect is. How is he dressed? What impression does he give in terms of mood, appearance, and demeanor?

Now, have the feminine aspect come out of the left side of the pelvic area and stand beside the male. Ask the same kinds of questions to determine what she looks like. The more balanced the person is, the more similar and compatible the masculine and feminine aspects. Ideally, both should be about the same age and be healthy and attractive. Ideally they are best friends. This is rarely the case unless the person has done a lot of therapy and has resolved most relationship issues. Sometimes one or both is very young, very old, sick, crippled, or somehow physically distorted and/or emotionally distressed. Sometimes the two snarl at each other in rage. Sometimes one is very old and the other is a child. Notice how the two aspects compare. They reflect any inner imbalances. The purpose of this exercise is to resolve the differences as best you can.

The next step is to get the two aspects to describe each other. One at a time, ask her what her impression is of him, what she likes and dislikes about him. The female is usually the feeler, so you can ask how she "feels" about him. Then ask the same questions of the male and learn his impressions of the female. The male is usually more of a thinker, so you can ask what he "thinks" about her. Get as much detail as possible. The object of the questions is to find the areas of conflict. Find where the imbalance lies.

Now it is time to get the two to talk with each other and begin to resolve their differences. Use your intuition and creativity as if you are an arbitrator in a dispute or negotiating the terms of a peace agreement. The goal is to get them to appreciate each other's positive qualities, to have compassion for each other's shortcomings, and to agree to be mutually supportive in healing any conflicts between them. They need to learn how to empower each other. You may need to start by getting them to feel safe and trust each other. They may need to explain to each other what each one needs and wants from the other. How can the male help the female, and vice versa? The goal is to get the two to become friends. As soon as they have come to an understanding and appreciation of each other, the dialog is complete. You can now have the person visualize the male and female embracing or dancing or making love in celebration of their new relationship with each other.

A total reconciliation and romantic ending is not always possible. The more incompatible the two aspects are, the less likely this is. Even in severe cases, chances are you will get them to at least hold hands. Do the best you can. Make as much progress as possible. This exercise can be repeated over and over through time to facilitate complete balance. Sometimes the two will be so angry that you will have to coax them even to look at each other. Perhaps that is all you can accomplish the first time. This is a good start. Any change is progress.

This is an easy exercise and incredibly beneficial and powerful. It can be done even with children.

The person subsequently should check in with "the couple" on a regular basis to continue the work if the two have not resolved their differences. Even after resolution, it is helpful to periodically check to see if the couple are continuing the compatibility and mutual respect. Any issues that arise can be negotiated and resolved internally rather than having to act them out in the "real world" through your relationship with your partner and the other people in your life.

SOUL RETRIEVAL

One of the wonderful techniques used to help people recall fragments of themselves is called soul retrieval. During different times of trauma throughout our lives, the pain can be so bad that we can fracture and pieces of our soul can break loose. Pieces of soul can break away any time from birth to the present, and these pieces of our soul have consciousness within them. Many times, this is why people feel so incomplete.

There is a way to retrieve these aspects of the self. This process can take a short time or a long time, depending on how many pieces have broken away. The result of the technique I will give will help you love and heal past memories and experiences, to create a sense of wholeness in yourself.

Soul Retrieval Technique

Have the person close his/her eyes and imagine being in a forest or park with big trees. Have the person select a large, beautiful tree. Tell him/her to walk into the tree and find an imaginary elevator that goes to the top of the tree. Once the person has reached the top, have him/her sit on a nice, strong branch and look up at the sky. Have the person ask the intuitive part of self to come out and sit beside him/her. Then have the person explain to the intuitive self that there are missing pieces that are necessary for living a healthy life. The intuitive self will be an instrument to help the person become whole.

Have the person ask the intuitive self to point out into the universe to where one of the missing fragments is. Ask the intuitive self if it is willing to go and bring this fragment back. If it agrees, have the person take the intuitive self by the hand, like a child or adolescent, and fly out into the universe to the area where the fragment resides. When they arrive, they will communicate with the fragment to find out why it left. Then they will communicate to the fragment that Earth is a safe and loving place to be and it is safe now to return. Usually the fragment will agree to come back. Have the three of them return together to the top of the tree. Have a ceremony in which the fragment and the intuitive self are brought back into the person's body. Have the person really feel a sense of completeness. Complete the visualization by having the person come back down the elevator and walk out of the tree, feeling whole.

If the fragment refused to come back, have the person tell the fragment it is loved and needed and he/she will be back later to talk with it again.

This technique can be done many times because there can be many, many lost parts of self. This technique also can be done on yourself.

REMOVING ENTITIES AND RELEASING ATTACHMENTS

The bodies surrounding Earth, composing her aura, are called planes. Just as we have a physical body and aura, so does Mother Earth. Her emotional body is the astral plane. There is a lower astral plane, mid astral plane, and higher astral plane. She also has higher, mid, and lower mental planes. Beyond that is her higher self - the soul and spirit of Earth which are being integrated currently in her ascension process.

ENTITIES

There are different kinds of entities, positive and nonpositive. Depending on the type, they reside in different planes. Examples of positive entities are masters, guides, and angels; they reside in Earth's higher self and beyond. Nonpositive entities, such as demons, reside in the lower astral plane. One kind of entity that can be either positive or nonpositive is earthbound spirits; these are people who died suddenly, often traumatically, while in a highly emotional state. There is a *bardo*, or bridge phase, that is a three-and-a half-day period following death when deceased friends, family, and a spiritual master such as Jesus or Buddha, wait to take the deceased into the light. Sometimes, due to the emotional state or trauma at the time of death, the person misses the *bardo*; these people think they are still alive and they become stuck in the astral plane. They are commonly referred to as ghosts. These lost souls are not necessarily lost forever. There are future opportunities for earthbound spirits to experience the *bardo*. Also there are living people and/or other helper entities whose work involves retrieving lost souls.

There also are dark-force beings that are ignorant and evil. They deliberately try to harm people because they are ill-intentioned. Sometimes they want to get even with people and/or to revenge the way they themselves died; for example, someone who was murdered. If someone is angry at the time of death, he/she can stay angry beyond life, come back in entity-form for revenge, and act out evil intentions through living people. This is commonly called possession.

Whoever energetically allows such an entity to come in can be possessed. Entities live off the life force of humans and can motivate people to do their bidding. Lower beings often frequent bars and other places with alcoholics and drug addicts. People under the influence of alcohol or drugs unknowingly expand and weaken their auric field to the point that they are easily penetrated. In addition, nonpositive entities thrive on the "high" induced by alcohol and/or drugs. Nonpositive entities can influence the behavior of the person they possess literally by whispering instructions into the person's ear, such as, "Kill that man now." A person in a state where he/she can be influenced often will act out such orders. Police files are full of such examples, like the Son of Sam who admitted that he "heard voices" directing him to kill.

There are also demons who focus on sex. They influence their host to perform perverse sexual activities or to act out sexual crimes, such as child abuse. There are also sexual entities who energetically have sex with people while they are sleeping. These are commonly called Incubus and Sucubus. Dark-force beings can attempt to possess us during sleep.

Mental institutions house many possessed people. They are not really sick. Instead, they are being ruled or overshadowed by entities who cause them to behave in ways that we define and categorize as "mental illness."

These nonpositive entities are beings you need to protect yourself from. As you become more and more healthy emotionally, and more advanced spiritually, your aura will become so resilient that you automatically will be protected because you can't be penetrated. In the meantime, practice the Protection Techniques given in chapter three.

Disease Entities

Another form of entity is a disease entity. These are entities we all create. There is an entity for each disease or affliction; for example, cancer entities, tuberculosis entities, fear entities, and depression entities. They are self-created entities. We create these entities out of our belief systems. A disease entity has its own consciousness. It helps create the disease in the body, then helps perpetuate that disease.

Cancer comes from self-hatred and a self-hatred entity is created. Arthritis has an entity that expresses rigidity. The hepatitis entity expresses anger in the liver. The obsessive entity affects the spleen. AIDS is a sexual-guilt entity. We create these entities out of our own thought forms.

Disease entities lodge in the body. Other entities, both positive and nonpositive, are in the aura. Many times, they attach themselves to us with big, thick cords that look like big tubes or ropes. Through these cords, these entities drain our energy. In *Psychic Self-Defense*, Dion Fortune compares the presence of an entity to the situation with two cars connected to one battery. There is not enough energy for both. To release yourself from the effect of such entities, there is a process, described below, that can be done to cut these cords.

Another form of entity is called "harpies." These are tiny energy forms that feel like they have teeth that bite. In fact, they do bite. They usually occur in an aura in groups or nests, like insects. They can be wiped off or pulled out energetically. Be sure to wash your hands after removing harpies.

We create or attract entities on a subconscious level. We create anger entities by being angry. If you think and feel anger long enough, that energy begins to gel. It is like a thought that takes form. Or anger can attract external angry astral entities. When you face the issues underlying your anger and clear this energy, the self-created anger entities such as hepatitis dissipate, and the external anger entities find another host. Like attracts like. Like creates like.

Attachments

There are also cords that attach us to people, places, and things. When these connections are unhealthy, they can drain our energy or dominate our lives. These unhealthy connections are called attachments. Attachments to people, places, or things include unhealthy relationships; rigid adherence to beliefs such as religious or political fanaticism; spending excessive time in bars; and addictions such as sex, alcohol, food, money, gambling, shopping, or any substance or activity that is mood-altering.

Every time two people have sex, cords of attachment form between them. You are connected to everyone you have ever been sexual with. During sex, you are therefore also connecting to the energy of everyone your partner ever has been sexual with. The good news is that these cords can be disconnected, releasing you from all past sexual partners.

Another form of attachment happens with people who have lost a loved one, but continue the relationship as if the person is still alive. This is a disservice to both parties; it not only keeps the living person from resuming a normal life, it also keeps the deceased person from moving on into the light.

The goal of spiritual growth with regard to attachments is to move into divine indifference and release attachment to all things. This does not mean giving up everything. It means release your attachment to things. You can have anything you want, anything at all. You just don't want to be attached to it. You don't want to need it in a dependent way. Your relationship to everything and everyone should be healthy. You don't want any person or thing to control you or drain your power. And you don't want to control or drain anyone else.

Technique for Releasing Attachments and Entities

The process is cutting the cords. This technique can be done on yourself or to facilitate another. Have the person close his/her eyes and call forth the masters, teachers, guides and angels to guide and protect him/her. The first step is to have the person state what to release. It is important to have the person talk about the relationship to this person, place, or thing, because a part of releasing is the understanding of how that unhealthy connection or habit has served the person. The next step is to have the person imagine or feel the attachment standing before him/her. Have the person describe what it looks or feels like, how he/she feels about it, and the relationship or agreement with the attachment. Have the person also feel where the cords are connected to the body. Some people actually visualize these cords and can give detailed descriptions of what they look like. Other people only feel or imagine pressure at the attachment sites. All impressions are valid.

Once the nature of an attachment has been identified, it is time to cut the cords and break the agreement. Have the person thank the attachment for the service it has provided (e.g., comfort, power, the need to feel connected), tell the object of attachment it is now time to leave. Have the person imagine taking a pair of scissors or a knife or machete or laser gun, any tool, and cutting all the cords very close to the body. After all the cords have been cut, have the person imagine sealing the wounds with light.

It is now time to send the object of the attachment away and into the light. Have the person call forth a divine being for assistance in this removal process. Have the person observe or imagine the object (or individual) moving further and further away until it can't be seen anymore and has been absorbed by the light of the spiritual plane. Then have the person imagine standing under a waterfall, with the water rushing through him/her, purifying every cell and particle of the being.

The attachment usually will try to reconnect. It is best to have this person repeat the cutting-of-the-cords visualization twice a day for at least two weeks.

This same attachment removal process can be used

to remove dark entities. However, in this case it is especially important to discuss the nature of the relationship between the person and each entity; each subconscious agreement with an entity is called a "contract." As with any contract, this agreement usually includes provisions that serve each party. For example, the entity will do things for the person in exchange for permission to live in the aura; the entity can psychically bring sexual partners, material things such as money or business opportunities, and success.

In the clearing process of dark entities, it is important for the person to talk with the entity and explore the terms of the contract. The person must be willing to give up the services that the entity has provided and, instead, trust that God will now provide. Once the contract is discussed, the person should tell the entity that the contract is broken. The person may even imagine burning the contract. At this point, cutting the cords can take place. In this case, due to the persistence of most dark entities, the cord-cutting visualization may need to be repeated twice daily for up to six months. If the entity is particularly persistent and still refuses to leave after six months, it probably will be necessary to perform an exorcism.

Following the use of this attachment removal technique, the person can experience grief or loss, as if losing a loved one through death. It is indeed a loss of someone or something. The loss could be a home the person decides to sell, or a pattern of behavior that has been a part of his/her life for a long time. It is normal to feel and experience such a change as a loss. The person may feel sad and cry, or feel disoriented while adjusting to the new energy status quo. If the situation involves releasing an attachment to a friend or family member who actually died, the person may begin grieving for the first time. The person should honor this need; the period of grieving could last six months or more, depending on the circumstances.

When we have been living our life in a certain way for a long period of time, it is often difficult to change our current situation. But in order to have a happy and full life, sometimes we must be willing to give up what is not healthy for us. All of the powerful mind-clearing techniques in this chapter are about change for the purpose of healing and personal growth. Whether you are releasing attachments, removing patterns, decoding the symbols of your subconscious mind, retrieving soul fragments, and/or re-parenting your inner child, it is important to be willing to move on. There is always someone or something better waiting for you. Be brave and trust spirit.

SIX

Other Ways to Improve the Quality of Your Life

CREATION AND MANIFESTATION

*t*hroughout all time, brilliant philosophers, theologians, and prophets have told us that what we think and feel creates our lives and the effect we have on everyone and everything around us. I agree. It is very important for us, as spiritual beings, to take responsibility for all of our actions.

We also are influenced by the thoughts and feelings of everyone and everything around us. For example, have you ever walked into a room feeling great; suddenly you felt depressed, angry, or suspicious? What happened? You were directly influenced by the thoughts and feelings of other people in the room. You took on someone else's reality.

The responsibility lies within you to be consciously aware that not all people come from a position of high integrity, balance, and unconditional love. It is your responsibility to protect yourself before going into a room full of people. Simply ask for the Christ light to surround and protect you. Second, you need to learn how to discern - from your emotional and spiritual chakras - whether it is your own emotional baggage or someone else's. It is up to you to remember what state of mind and emotions you were in when you entered the room, how you felt when you walked in. If you have taken on the thoughts and emotions of other people, simply say to yourself mentally, *I release all negativity from myself now.* By doing this, you will take back your power and move back into the state of happiness and balance you were in initially.

Have you ever noticed that the things we fear are often the very things we pull into our lives? This happens because our thoughts and feelings energize and feed fear. If we energize a fear enough, we actually create a negative scenario and draw it into our life. A perfect example occurred years ago when I was married. Regularly for two years, I accused my husband of cheating on me. Finally, he came to me and said, "You got what you wanted. I just slept with another woman. Are you happy now?" This was back in my darker days; so my solution was to sleep with his best friend. It was a destructive experience; because not just our immediate family was harmed, but so were the other families. We had drawn them into our own drama that was manifesting and playing out my irrational fears. We divorced shortly thereafter; the trust was gone and we could not restore it. This was a big lesson for me. It changed my life and forced me to find out why I felt so insecure and jealous. After years of introspection I realized it was not about my husband at all. It was about my own feelings of unworthiness and lack of trust in men because my father had cheated on my mother. And guess what, my mother had retaliated by having sex with the husband of the woman my dad was having an affair with.

Thoughts and feelings have forms. Some people with psychic vision can see them. As soon as the form has been created out of the mental or emotional body, this form stays in the aura for a while, then moves into the collective consciousness. These can be either loving thoughts and feelings, or fearful thoughts and feelings. So, we make the choice.

As human beings, we have been programmed at our core to see ourselves as victims. Most of the population believes that somebody is "doing something to them." It is our responsibility, as spiritually conscious people, to accept responsibility for our creations and thereby lift the consciousness of ourselves and the human race. One statement of "I hate you," negates one hundred "I love you's."

It is important for us to consciously have loving thoughts and prayers constantly flowing from our mind and emotions. We must have the awareness that we are a co-creator and we do affect the consciousness of thousands of people. This is why we keep hearing and reading that we should think positively.

The following statement seems appropriate. It relates to the mirroring process of magnetically pulling into our lives people with the negative characteristics that we have ourselves and therefore are intolerant of.

> Anyone or anything with whom or which I have a relationship will act out for me my subconscious thoughts. When I change my subconscious thoughts, the things, conditions or person's behavior changes!
>
> - Author Unknown

A practice I use frequently is to examine my own feelings of dislike or anger toward another. I go inside myself and find what it is in me that stimulates these feelings. I realize I have obviously drawn this person to me to mirror my own negativity. The issues always belong to me as well.

GOD LIVES IN THE MIND

In understanding that we all came from the same God, it should seem obvious that we are all made up of the same spiritual essence - in our atoms, cells, and all parts of our being. If this is so, the God energy lives in our being, mind, emotional body, mental thoughts, and physical body. Just a few weeks ago, I saw a beautiful video workshop of an Indian saint. She said, "Be careful what you say, because the Lord lives in your mind, as he also lives in all parts of you." At that moment, for the first time, I really understood that God does hear all my thoughts and words. As I walk around talking to myself, either out loud or in my mind, some of the words are swear words. And my godself hears every one of them.

The bad thing about this is that our thoughts and feelings create our reality: the body we have, our habits, allergies, fantasies, and masks. In other words, what we think is who we are. Our subconscious minds take in everything that is said as truth, especially things that are spoken out loud. The subconscious does not have the discernment to know if something is coming from us or from someone else.

It occurred to me that all of the swear words coming out of my mouth were not only being heard by God, but I also was perpetuating the energy behind these words - fear, anger, and doom. So, now when I catch myself swearing, I correct the words immediately. And, lo and behold, my vocabulary is becoming "clean." Clean thoughts, clean mind. Clean mind, clean reality. For an exercise, start listening to your inner dialog and begin deleting the negative words and replacing them with positive words.

THE WITNESS

We all know that we have a higher and lower self. At some point in the development of our awareness, we begin to observe our own behavior. We move into what I call the "witness." We are able to objectively observe ourselves and our interactions with others. Before we move into the witness position, we are only able to see the world through our own perspective. Moving into the witness position is a process. It occurs step by step. The first step that leads toward the witness position is being able to review past behavior and realize that you have harmed others and/or yourself. You begin to judge yourself. And you are now able to feel remorse and guilt. This step normally occurs in the middle to late twenties. Those who don't ever get to this step have no guilt or conscience and can be labeled sociopathic personalities.

People who remain at the judging state are able to feel guilt, but are not able to understand the dynamics of what happened, so they are unable to correct the situation and are unable to learn from it. More importantly, they are not able to accept responsibility for their behavior, or their part in creating the drama. Instead, they seek to blame others. They also feel they have no choice. Life happens to them. This is also the victim position. People hang onto this position for dear life. A large percentage of the population functions from this level.

For those who are able to move beyond this, and move further toward the witness position, the next step is to become mentally aware of human dynamics and have enough insight and understanding to be able to see how they could have behaved differently. From this perspective, people are able to learn from past mistakes. This does not mean they are able to change their behavior as it happens. However, they are able to review situations and apologize, if appropriate. They are also able to realize how they could have behaved differently in a more positive way. For someone at this step, it is helpful to ask, "How would Jesus, or any divine being, have handled this situation?" Or, "How would I have wanted to be treated myself in this situation?"

The final step in moving into the witness position is when you watch yourself and realize - while the interaction is taking place - that you have a choice in how to behave in a more mature, sensitive, and loving way. This entails not getting lost in the emotions of the situation. It is a more mental and detached position. More importantly, it is a spiritual position. You are operating from your higher self. It can also be a very important place to be because, if you catch yourself operating out of habit or old familiar patterns, you now have the power to stop, admit your limitations, and change your behavior. This can be very scary at first. It may involve admitting you are wrong. It may involve telling the truth. It may involve wounding your own pride.

The consequences also can involve losing friends who are not able to adjust to your new way of communicating and interacting. From your new perspective, which is unconditionally loving, you have compassion and understanding for everyone in your life. However, the other person(s) may no longer be comfortable interacting with you and they may choose to find other friends at their level. The good news is you will find new friends. You will magnetically draw to you people who are also able to function from the witness position and take responsibility for their own actions and creations. These people will be of a much higher vibration than the friends who have gone away.

After you have moved into this new consciousness

of being the witness in your everyday life, you are operating more from the higher self and are able to reap other benefits of this level, such as forgiveness and acceptance.

Following is a technique to help you start practicing living from the witness position. Imagine you are sitting in a theater in the balcony looking down at the stage. You are watching yourself and another person interact. You are able to see your part in the drama. You can create anything. You can change anything. You can edit anything. And from a non-judgmental perspective, you can objectively make these changes. Your mind will infuse this new way of communication like a new positive program, replacing the old negative behavior. Practice doing this at least once a day. You are reprogramming your mind. After your mind understands what you are doing, it will begin to help you by creating a higher standard of living for you. This is an exciting way to live each day. From the witness position you know you are the author of your life. You can begin experiencing more positive outcomes. And you created them!

GIVING TO YOURSELF FIRST

This is the most basic of all the principles in our spiritual growth, yet this is usually the last thing we do. Most spiritual people, especially healers, are givers. They are usually the last to receive love and healing for themselves.

We are in a time of healing on the planet. With the millenium change, our global consciousness is shifting. The desire to become whole is very strong now. Healers are natural channels for healing energy and unconditional love.

This all seems like everything is balanced and in order, and it is, if the healer receives in as much light, love and abundance as he/she gives out. Unfortunately, many healers and givers get stuck in the mode of giving and forget about themselves.

We know that helping others makes us feel good. However, if we don't receive back in an equal amount, our lower chakras are not being cleared or transmuted. Self-worth, self-esteem, self-love, and self-support (including financial) are put on the back burner if we give too much and receive too little. Unless we balance the scales and allow others to give to us and help us to heal, we are hiding or avoiding the negative desire-level feelings and disorders within ourselves. These disorders can include self-destructive habits or addictions. Healers who ignore their own needs and unresolved issues, usually have serious baggage. They cannot "walk the talk." This is why so many healers are unable to support themselves financially. They have not cleared their own issues.

My first experience with learning to receive was very painful. When I came back from a trip to India in 1988 after visiting Sai Baba's ashram, I became sick with hepatitis. Chronic hepatitis had been lying dormant in my liver for twenty years from injecting drugs in the sixties. The virus was activated by Sai Baba's power, the kundalini. Being in his presence changed my life forever. At first I thought that I had contracted the disease in India. But when I was back in Denver, the doctor told me I had hepatitis "C," and I knew it was from the past. Hepatitis is a debilitating disease with symptoms such as major fatigue, nausea, vomiting, depression, physical pain, and emotional rage (anger and rage are stored in the liver). I had a roommate at the time who was a healer doing an apprenticeship with me. It was incredibly difficult for me to allow her to care for me. She had to feed and bath me and generally care for me as an invalid. This pushed all my buttons. I had always been a very independent person. This situation triggered all my dependence and control issues and fears. I was forced to surrender control of my life and allow another human being to take care of me. This experience was timely and important. It was a major step in my growth. In going through this experience, I came to fully understand how out of balance I had been in giving and receiving, and how angry and resentful I was about that imbalance.

As soon as I healed the hepatitis, I consciously began giving to myself. I had to train myself to receive. The first thing I did was to stop buying lunch for everybody. I stopped paying everybody's way. This was very threatening to my ego and I felt out of control. I realized that a major reason for giving all the time was to keep people in my life. Out of my unworthiness issues, I was afraid they would leave if I didn't pay them to stay. And some people did leave. Those who were only in my life to use and take advantage of me left when the gravy train stopped. However, many people stayed and gave to me. These people are still my friends today and are valuable in my life.

There are many ways to give to yourself: treat yourself to a hot bath with candles and soft music, buy yourself some flowers, send yourself a card that says "I love you." One of the main gifts I have given to myself for the past twelve years is a weekly massage. This heals my body and, since I perceive it as a gift, it also heals me emotionally.

It is important to learn to set boundaries and say "no." If someone asks for a favor and you feel uncomfortable, there are several ways to handle this. One, buy yourself some time to think about it. I usually tell the person, "Let me sleep on it. I'll let you know tomorrow." If, after you've pondered the request, you still feel uncomfortable, you either can just say no, or you can try to balance the energy by agreeing to do the request in exchange for something from the other person.

It is also important to allow others to give to you. In my case, I had to learn to allow others to pay for my lunch.

This sounds easy, but it was very difficult to do. If someone offers you a gift, accept it graciously, without feeling that you owe that person something in return.

A healthy person understands that giving unconditionally also includes receiving - but not necessarily to and from the same person. You may give to person "A" who gives to person "B" who gives back to you or to another person. The universe will make sure that you are reimbursed in one way or another. Balanced energy always comes full circle. This is the law of cause and effect in the universe.

YOUTHING IN THE NEW MILLENIUM

As we move through the decades, we are inspired by all the new products on the market that promise to make us look and feel stronger and younger. But it is tough to decide which product to buy, which health club to join. There are so many decisions to make and only so much time and money to go around.

What if I were to tell you that, while it is fun and entertaining to try out all the new methods and products, "youth" does not come in a bottle. Youth comes from our attitude and self-image. In other words, we are as young as our mind and emotions perceive us to be. You've probably heard the saying, "You are what you eat!" Maybe you've seen the T-shirt that has a picture of a gross looking pizza on it with that caption. Well this is somewhat true, but there's more to the story than just this basic statement. In fact, if you have cleared away enough false illusions and beliefs about your appearance, it could be a greater truth that "You are what you see in the mirror."

We all know that sometimes we look in the mirror and see a young, beautiful, and vibrant person. The next day, we look into the same mirror and the person we see looking back at us is perhaps older, with a wrinkled face, and saggy jowls and skin. What happened overnight? It seems to be a complete mystery! The truth is that our self-image changed and the second time we looked in the mirror we weren't feeling very confident or energetic. Consequently, the image we were sending out to the mirror - and to the world - was that of an older person. It's that simple.

I learned a technique several years ago about how to look attractive even if I wasn't feeling pretty, thin, or young. I'm going to pass this secret on to you. The person who taught me this technique had no idea how important this simple exercise would be in my life. Believe me, it has been an incredible tool for saving my relationships.

Exercise

It is important to understand that this is an intuitive exercise and you will be using your imagination to create an image of yourself that is young, fit, vibrant, and attractive. An easy way to do this is by going through old pictures of yourself and finding a look you would like to have now. Of course, if you are middle-aged, it is not appropriate to try to look seventeen. Be reasonable in your choice. When you find the picture, study the facial features and the youthful energy in the stance. Feel the passion that you had when the picture was taken and imagine that you are that age again. If you don't have a picture, imagine yourself at a more desirable and younger age. Start practicing standing more erect and feel the engine starting to accelerate inside your body. Feel yourself at this younger age and feel it in every cell of your body. Take a few breaths and imagine this image covering your body like a garment. You may feel butterflies in your stomach, or you may feel like pounding on your chest and making sounds like Tarzan. In fact, the reason he pounded on the upper part of his chest and made that animal sound was to stimulate the thymus gland and give himself great energy.

The next step is to test out your new look. Go to a public place, take a moment to sit and visualize and feel this younger image - until it feels truly a part of you. Now, begin watching and studying people. Choose a person you see as attractive, but maybe quite a few years younger. Choose someone you ordinarily would never even consider flirting with. Stand up straight, take a deep breath and feel the youthful passion running through your veins. Make sure you are wearing the "younger garment" and break into a broad smile. Watch the response you get. If, by any chance, this person stops and you have the opportunity to have a conversation, ask this person to guess your age. The response probably will surprise you.

Keep practicing. Practice every day, in different settings. Another opportune time to practice this exercise is when you wake up with your mate in the morning, with your hair sticking up and pillow marks all over your face. Slip into your "younger garment" and feel young through and through. What follows may be a very pleasant surprise!

This technique eventually will become a natural part of your awareness. Finally this will be the new you. Each time you look in the mirror you will see a more vital and youthful person looking back at you, and you'll want to start dressing this new self with fun clothes and brighter colors. It really does become a way of life. If your ego is trying to sabotage you by saying "You are really old and you are making a fool out of yourself," talk back to the voice by saying, "No!" Then say a positive affirmation three times, something like "I am young, healthy, deserving, and vital." Always state the affirmation in present time. Say, "I am (such and such)." Never say, "I will be (such and such)." The subconscious mind takes everything literally. If you say, "I will be (such and such)," you are programming yourself for the future, and you do not live in the future, you live in the present. Start practicing, and as you grow younger day by day, you will be thrilled by your creation and the manifestation of the new you. Before long all parts of yourself will believe you are really young and healthy. Life is fun! Enjoy!

CAREER TRANSITIONING

In my practice, approximately one third of the clients who come to me for counseling are somewhere in the process of career transition. It is important for you to know that such a career transition is not as big and scary as you may feel. It is just a whole life change (chuckle).

For people who know that their current work is not satisfying, and who know they want something different, but don't know what that new work should be, there is an easy way to find out. Think about what your own dream was earlier in life, or when you were a child. Examine these work situations to determine the type of work involved. Did you want to work for someone else? Or did you want to be the boss? Did you want to work alone? Did you want to work with people? Or did you want to work with technology and/or machines? Did you want to work indoors or outdoors? Look for the general patterns that your dreams revealed. Once you have determined the type of working situation you wanted, that becomes the basis to build a new career and a new life.

The second step is to examine what professions and jobs will exist in the future, and which will meet your financial needs. Choose one or more to explore that are both practical and that satisfy your dreams for an ideal work situation.

The third step is to use your imagination to help you

evaluate your options. Imagine you are sitting in one of the work situations you have been considering. Feel everything around you. Smell everything. How does your body feel? Ask your higher self to show you a red light (meaning "STOP! This probably is not for you." Or, "Something is missing.") Or a green light (meaning "GO! This choice has good potential for you."). Do this same exercise with all of your options. Make note of which one(s) feel right. You may visit these scenarios many times in your imagination; you will be able to eliminate the less desirable ones.

The fourth step is to do the groundwork. What schooling or training do you need? Most people believe they need a formal education, perhaps even an advanced degree, to perform many of the jobs available today. This is not necessarily so. Many, many people take basic skills plus a positive attitude and desire for success and become successful at whatever they choose to do. So, before you enroll in a lengthy education program, investigate other options. For example, go to a bookstore or library and get all of the newsletters and magazines, and study the ads and compare the costs for courses. You can study to be a Reiki Master for $10,000 in a two-year program; or you can take a weekend training course for $95 and also be certified as a Reiki Master. The same thing applies to hypnosis training and many other modalities. Obviously, the $10,000 two-year program offers much more than the weekend. How much training do you need? If one program is too much and one is not enough, find something in-between. The point is, the options are endless. There are many inexpensive courses and workshops offered through free universities, community colleges, personal teachers, apprenticeship programs, etc. Take as many of these classes as you can. All knowledge is useful.

Know that it is never too late to fulfill your dream

and to find satisfying work. I consider my spiritual awakening in the early 1980s as the beginning of a new life within this lifetime. I started over completely, as will anyone who goes through such a major transition. I realized that I was at a crossroads. I needed to make a decision about which way to go. I could stay in the "system" forever, working for other people in traditional jobs. Or I could create my own career from my passionate creative Self. In looking at each road, the traditional job felt more secure, but less satisfying.

I believed it would be hard to create my own profession and title, especially since at that point I didn't even know what it would be. But I also knew to ask God for omens and signs about what my spiritual work should be. I started watching every day for any little sign or suggestion, even if it was something someone was saying on television. I remained open during this period. I prayed and meditated each day, asking for guidance.

In 1982 I found an advertisement in a newsletter for a woman in Denver who gave psychic readings. I immediately made an appointment to see her. After the two-hour reading, I walked out of her house knowing that this was what I wanted to do. So I announced to all of my friends, "I want to be a psychic." Of course, they all thought I was crazy and laughed it off. But that was my goal. Through a friend, I found a psychic school that was taught many years ago in Denver. It exposed me to all the basics; but I realized that none of it was new to me, that I already perceived the world through psychic eyes. I also learned that my universal way of thinking, which my formal education in psychology had labeled as "cause and effect," was similar to the basic laws of right and wrong and the basic tenants of most religions. For example, "Do unto others as you would have others do unto you." Once again, my philosophy was already spiritual in essence. I did not need to be taught the standards and principles upon which I would base my future work. I simply needed to acknowledge what I already knew.

The development of my psychic gifts led me first to trance channeling. This happened spontaneously in the middle of the night. Then, through the Tibetan Foundation, I moved into conscious channeling. I also studied healing techniques for a few years. By the 1990s I had stopped channeling the messages (i.e., I stopped allowing the divine masters to speak through me by taking over my consciousness and my body). Instead, I now receive the messages by inviting the masters to stand beside me and speak to me.

In 1993 I made an additional transition so I could help "main stream" clients as well as my spiritual clients. I now practice psychotherapy with "main stream" clients with the help of a wise and wonderful supervisor, Dr. James A. Sharon, Ed.D., who is a licensed psychologist. This is a good example of being flexible and checking out options. I work with many people who have emotional disorders, with children, and with other unique cases. I use traditional counseling techniques with them. However, while they are doing an exercise with eyes closed, I covertly check out their auras and I use my intuitive gifts to guide the sessions.

Not all people are meant to be entrepreneurial, but if you feel that you would do well using your own creativity and strength to start your own business, then perhaps it would be a valuable experience for you to make a plan. Start with your idea and build on that. Piece by piece your business should fall into place. You must be determined and keep it simple at first, staying focused and contemplative. Call on the Divine and always know that the universe supports you and will help you, but it needs to know what your intentions are.

Other Ways to Improve the Quality of Your Life

SEVEN

Extraterrestrials

Since the 1940s, there has been controversy about whether or not extraterrestrials (ET's) are real or not. At that time, the existence of these beings was questionable. However, now surveys show that eighty-five percent of the population believe that ET's do exist. Many people, like scientists, suggest that it is arrogant and self-centered to believe that we humans are the only species in all of creation. In my opinion, we can assume that we are not alone.

There have been many different types of ET's reported. Evidently the loving light beings, like those depicted in the movie Cocoon, allow us to feel safe and comfortable and are the most desirable to have around.

We also have the Greys. These are the ET's who reportedly do abductions and experiments on humans. They also purportedly do animal mutations. Whitley Striber wrote about the Greys in his book, *Communion.* I attended a lecture by him in the late 1980s in Los Angeles. He spoke of several different types of ET's.

At that time, I had been having visitations by a very large lizard-looking being. He would come and stand in my room each night. I always felt he was my protector. He told me he was named Pisarius. Because I am clairvoyant, I was able to see him. His nature was gentle and loving.

Whitley Striber spoke of the lizard beings in his lecture. I asked many questions because he was speaking about a species with which I was familiar. I don't remember the specifics, but I did not get the impression from Striber that this is a harmful being or species.

After the lecture, when I went into the hall, a small boy about eight years old, came up to me and showed me his drawing of the lizard being that was a companion to him. I looked at the drawing and said, "That's my lizard!" He replied, "No, that's mine!" This validated for me that I wasn't crazy or making it up.

A few years later in 1995 a friend of mine, Tashira Taichi-ren (author of *What is Lightbody?*), and I were talking one night. I asked her about the lizard beings because she was an ET enthusiast. She informed me that there are two different types of lizard beings, some with scales and some with slick, shiny skin. Evidently the ones with scales are the spiritual ones. The shiny ones are supposedly dark forces. My lizard visitor was one of the scaly ones.

Until I was able to see very clearly psychically, I would see beings moving though the house every day. Some of these were ET's. I had to use my feeling nature to determine whether they were friendly. Now that I can see more clearly, I am able to determine their nature visually. It is very rare for me to see dark beings.

ET's are not my specialty, but of those I am familiar with, the light-loving beings include the Pleiadians, the scaly lizards, and the small, tan-colored beings with the long fingers and big eyes (the species that reportedly crashed at Roswell, New Mexico, in July 1948, and that subsequently was depicted in the movies *Close Encounters of the Third Kind* and *ET Go Home*).

Obviously, since ET's are here on the planet, most of them came by spacecraft. I have seen many craft. In about 1985 I was a member of a group of UFO watchers in Denver. We would go to the mountains, lie on blankets on the ground on summer evenings, and watch the sky. In the beginning I thought it was fun but had no validity. However, once I began seeing the UFOs myself, it was very clear to me that we are not alone. I was shown a craft moving across the sky at great speed. I commented, "That was a satellite." The other person said, "Oh, really? Then what are all the other lights going back and forth on the busy 'highway' up there?" As soon as I knew how to look for them, I would see ten or twenty every night.

EIGHT

Kundalini

*K*undalini existed long before us. It is a force, an electrical power that permeates everything. It is alive in all things - rocks, plants, and, yes, even us. The Hindus regard kundalini as the Divine Mother. Kundalini has been acknowledged as the divine life force in many cultures and religions. It is known in China as *Chi*, in Japan as *Ki*, in the Christian religion as the Holy Spirit or Holy Ghost, in Indonesia as *Petara*, in Hebrew as *Ruach*, and the list goes on. Varying degrees of knowledge of this incredible force are interwoven throughout many religions and philosophies. The power of kundalini can be found any place where God is found, because the most profound thing that this great force embodies is love.

Within our universe and cosmos there are grids that are called ley lines. When people fly across the world, they fly over ley lines and end up with jet lag. These lines, made of energy, create a massive grid that looks like a giant spider web. The web connects everything together at a subtle or invisible level. Kundalini current travels along these ley lines and down onto the earth and into our electromagnetic fields (auras). If you are clear in body, mind, emotions, and spirit, you receive great benefits from this current.

There is also an inner aspect of kundalini that is not very well-known. This aspect has been acknowledged in Mystery Schools all over the world where the secrets of spiritual enlightenment have been the primary focus of their philosophy. The Hindus portray this inner aspect as a serpent coiled up three-and-a-half times at the base of the spine. It is a wonderful, powerful energy that lies dormant in the human body until awakened. The awakening can happen spontaneously as we begin actively working on our spiritual growth. This probably happens because the person has had kundalini risings in prior incarnations.

In other cases, kundalini can be deliberately awakened by a master (saint) or guru. Following the awakening, the master guides and helps these people continue on their spiritual path. The master facilitates the movement of the rising kundalini and helps the process of the initiate by removing the karmic blocks from the *sushumna nadi* (the subtle energy highway up and down the spine).

The kundalini energy is both vital and loving and can heal all things, including emotional wounds, mental traumas, and physical diseases. But, most importantly, as the kundalini rises up the spine, it opens and clears the chakras and expands consciousness. It is a major tool on the path to enlightenment. It is this inner aspect of kundalini that this chapter covers.

The masculine aspect of kundalini is hot and is known in eastern countries as *Shiva*. The feminine aspect is known as *Shakti* and her rays are cool and healing. The Tibetans use kundalini to test disciples and their power. For instance, some masters in Tibet have their disciples or monks put on a wet sheet and sit in a cold cave. Whoever dries the sheet the fastest with the body temperature has the most kundalini power.

Our goal as a spiritual initiate is to take this inner energy of kundalini to the highest possible level and continue to connect higher and higher until we access our higher self and function from this level all the time. At these high levels, we experience only unconditional love. Kundalini truly is a spiritual energy.

However, kundalini usually doesn't become active within us until we have done enough physical, emotional, and mental clearing. The kundalini brings wisdom and insight with it, so you must be ready to handle this knowledge and these truths about yourself and God before they are presented to you. Once you are relatively clear, then the energy can flow through you without hitting major blocks of resistance and causing major trauma. At this point, your higher self may guide you to find an enlightened kundalini master and/or assist you in raising this energy up your spine yourself. I believe the process is slower when you do it without a master.

KUNDALINI ENERGY HEALING

Kundalini has been sought for thousands of years because of its power to bring body, mind, and spirit back into a healed state. The most powerful healers run a lot of kundalini through their bodies and hands into others. Kundalini is said to move up from the base of the spine and out the top of the head after traveling through each chakra in the body. As it uncoils, the kundalini makes its way up the spine through the aura in a channel that is called the *sushumna*. This avenue, or *nadi*, is like the elevator up and down the spine. As the kundalini travels through each chakra, it purifies the negative qualities and magnifies the positive gifts. It also purifies the body as it goes through all organs, bones, glands, muscles, and out into the aura. You begin to heal, because the kundalini has its own innate intelligence and knows exactly where to travel in the body to purify you.

Kundalini is a powerful healing force that is capable of healing emotional disorders, mental traumas, and physical diseases such as cancer, diabetes, and heart disease. I personally am a testament to many chronic diseases that have been healed and bones repaired by kundalini. The major diseases I have healed in my body include cancer and chronic bronchitis. In addition, I now have a relatively small amount of pain in my body, considering all the broken bones, surgeries, and diseases I have experienced.

Now, I will not tell you that this healing process is always comfortable for all people, because sometimes it isn't. Sometimes people have what seem to be adverse reactions when kundalini *shakti* is present. Dramatic change happens as the positive energy pushes out the negative, low-vibration masses that can be disease or disease in the making. This can cause the cells to fill with fluid and begin to drain the negative matter out of the body in natural eliminative ways. You can experience cold or flu symptoms such as a runny nose, fever, fatigue, and/or nausea. You may think you are sick, but actually you are clearing after being exposed to the healing power of kundalini.

Also, if one or more chakras are not completely opened, the kundalini will find its way around. As it does, it may send a sharp charge over to the side of your sacrum or down through your legs, or around your ribs or wherever the blockage is located. This can result in muscle spasm, pain, headache, *kriya* (sharp jerky movements or sounds), swollen extremity, or flu symptoms from releasing toxins. These are all part of the purification process. The difference between regular healing and kundalini healing is that kundalini is much more powerful; it creates faster release of the old disease and negative energy from the body. After you recover, the result, of course, is greater health in the body and mind because you have released the nonpositive energy from your system and you are now clearer. Some people do not have any of these extreme reactions.

In addition, as part of the purification process, you will outgrow many of your harmful habits and behaviors. You may naturally give up cigarettes or ice cream or people who no longer serve your highest good. This is good news, because your health and life will improve. In the process, you will miss your old friends and habits and you probably will need to grieve for their loss. This can be physically, emotionally, and mentally painful. But this is true with all growth experiences.

This healing and enlightenment process can take a long time. But remember, it has taken a lifetime, probably more than one, to build all of your negative, destructive habits. The fabulous news is that kundalini is the fastest way to remove negativity. In the long run, you experience health, happiness, love, joy, and bliss. I feel that's a pretty good trade-off.

MY EXPERIENCES WITH KUNDALINI

Remembering back over many years of hair-raising moments and instances of great strength during life-threatening experiences, I know now that kundalini has been active in me for many years. I just didn't know what this "special inner energy" was. I can remember several experiences throughout my life when kundalini saved me. For example, one night years ago I was drinking in a neighborhood bar and had gotten into an argument with a very large woman. After leaving the bar I was walking through the parking lot to my car and heard footsteps coming up behind me. I knew it was the large woman by the heaviness of the feet hitting the ground. The last thing I remember was reaching directly over my shoulders and grabbing this person and throwing her down in front of me without turning around. My roommates and my son have never forgotten that night. I came to my senses after securing her physically on the ground.

Kundalini can give you great strength as it spontaneously takes over for the sake of survival. You may suggest that this is a natural reaction to an adrenaline rush, but I have had both and they are quite different. In *The Kundalini Experience, Psychosis or Transcendence*, Dr. Lee Sannella describes an eighty-year-old woman lifting a 2000-pound car to pull a child out from underneath. What caused this phenomenon? Adrenaline or kundalini? Maybe one, or both.

My first conscious experience with kundalini was dramatic and occurred in the early 1980s. As I mentioned in "Patrisha's Story," my autobiography, a man came to Denver teaching kundalini and enlightenment. I didn't consciously have a clue what all this meant, but I was drawn night after night to his lectures. As I sat there, I would hallucinate and feel an odd stimulating sensation sweeping up and down my spine. It was thrilling. He asked us to meditate with him and said he might levitate. He told us to keep our eyes closed. Well, of course, I peeked. I saw a huge orange light around his body and what appeared to be an enormous fountain of orange-golden light. I was shocked. There were sparks flying around him and I looked down at my own left arm and saw lavender lines of light like branches from a tree. I now know that those were my acupuncture meridians. This was incredible. I felt unified with God.

At one point, he told us to open our eyes so he could look each one of us in the eye and transfer *shakti*. I wondered how he would do that in a dark room. But, soon I noticed two lines of light coming from his eyes going into one person after the other. By the time he reached me, I was so spiritually altered that I didn't need much transference of light. He looked into my eyes and I didn't remember anything for a few minutes. I went to another place. Then the lights in the room came up and it was question-and-answer time. I'm sure people were annoyed with me because I had a thousand questions. I was hungry for information about kundalini. I knew this was what I needed for my spiritual enlightenment. I wanted more.

He encouraged us to meditate and chant. I was already a meditator, but after this I spent many more hours in meditation each day (probably too many) and experienced incredible visions and sounds. Then one night, while I was chanting, breathing and meditating, all of a sudden the muscles in my legs, abdomen, chest, and neck bunched up in spasms. I heard what sounded like a train going through my head, or a rocket roaring up my spine. There was an explosion in my head that sounded like a thousand bones breaking. Then there was a tremendous explosion of light and I dropped into the deepest state I had ever been in. It scared me; but as I jumped up and stood there shaking, I realized it was a kundalini rising that I had been reading so much about. I tried to bring it back, but I did not have a similar recurrence until I was in India a few years later. Now I know that my experience was so extreme because my spine was so blocked that the mighty kundalini had to rise like a train or rocket to work its way through the first time. Today, I have similar experiences, but not as extreme. I feel a warm fluid, like a river, moving through my back and limbs. It is very gratifying and peaceful.

The next day, however, my right eye was swollen shut. Now I know that the kundalini wasn't able to get through on the right side. I had to reduce the intensity of my meditations for a while so the energy could flow freely through all of my chakras.

I was also lifting about an inch off the floor while walking. My dreams were ecstatic, all about God and filled with joy. It wasn't long after that I began awakening each morning at four-thirty, standing in the middle of the room in odd postures that I now know were *mudras* (yoga postures), and I would be talking out loud (channeling). To learn more about channeling, kundalini and enlightenment, I subsequently joined the Tibetan Foundation, a group of channelers; and later traveled to India to study kundalini with the saints and gurus, such as Sai Baba.

Kundalini is a good friend to my body now. I can feel it moving or working to clear something out. Sometimes it feels like a poker or a serpent unwinding at the base of my spine; or I may notice the smell of flowers and know that kundalini has opened my third eye; or I may experience bliss and giggle for no apparent reason. Other times, I am filled with such love and compassion for humankind, animals, or nature that tears come to my eyes from the opening of my heart. Kundalini is so very mysterious and intoxicating, and yet so practical. When I am filled with the Goddess Kundalini, she won't lead me astray. She's my automatic pilot. She stimulates and facilitates my common sense and intuitive nature, and I stay in sync with God and the universe. I am so grateful that my inner God guided me to this path.

KUNDALINI - MYTHS, FEARS, AND DANGERS

There are several warnings and myths about kundalini that should be addressed. On the Internet, there is a lot of negative information about it. I can understand people being afraid of something they cannot see and something that is intangible. But if you are gentle with yourself and you allow kundalini to ascend your spine and through your body, it will take care of you on its own. However, if you force it, you can harm yourself physically and psychologically. So, be practical and, if you have concerns, see a guru. Many gurus travel the United States: Ananda Ma, Amachi, Gurumayi, Mother Mira, and Ram Dass (although he calls himself a teacher).

People fear the sexual aspects of kundalini. If the area of the first and second chakras is blocked, you could be sexually stimulated; and if you don't clear these chakras, you may act out lower passions. Always take kundalini into the heart and ask it to purify you. Remember, the lower chakras have lower passions until purified. The higher chakras also have passions, but they are not the desire level. The crown chakra is the connection to God. If you concentrate only on the crown chakra, generally you will be out of your body most of the time rather than experiencing being human. It is important that the kundalini move through all of your chakras.

The healthiest way to bring kundalini into its vital state in your body is through prayer, meditation, and breath work. There are simple ways to breathe that stimulate the energy. Many are used in yoga. Several examples are presented below as exercises.

I thank God each day for my intuitive vision that enables me to see peoples' auras. I am able to facilitate and help them clear blocked areas so the kundalini can move freely. If your goal is God-consciousness, and you yearn for enlightenment more than anything in life, you can't get hurt with kundalini as long as you are gentle. Moderation and common sense are important. The results depend on your intent. If your goal is the seeking of self-realization, and you are loving and pure in your intent, kundalini will guide you sweetly and smoothly.

SOME EXAMPLES OF THE IMPACTS OF KUNDALINI

I've shared my story. Now I will give a few other examples, involving five participants in my kundalini workshops.

Nancy's Story

Nancy's story is similar to many that involve health issues. She took my kundalini workshop and was thrilled with the power she felt. She immediately dropped twenty pounds, because the kundalini stimulates the metabolism. However, about two weeks later she called and said her doctor had diagnosed her with a hopeless case of diabetes. She had been diagnosed decades before, but for the past twenty years the disease had been dormant. I always counsel people to do what their doctors say and to have regular medical check-ups in addition to any alternative methods they practice. But I also told her that in my experience the kundalini moves disease out of the body. She should continue to take her insulin, but also should be aware that this could be a healing crisis. Kundalini is known for surfacing old diseases that have been dormant for years. However, she was convinced that the kundalini had re-stimulated her diabetes. So I said, "Okay, but please keep me informed of your progress, because I do care what happens to you." I didn't hear from her for one-and-a-half years. She called and said, "Guess what, you were right." The diabetes had left her body. It took the kundalini one-and-a-half years to clear her pancreas. It probably wouldn't have taken that long if she had understood that the disease was on the way out of her body, instead of believing that it was on its way in. Nancy no longer has diabetes.

John's Story

John came to a kundalini workshop because his mate wanted him there. He thought he would just tolerate all of us who were so into the energy and seeking to move deeper and deeper into the heart. The goal of the workshop was for all of us to become unconditionally loving toward ourselves and humankind. John thought nothing was happening to him, and he didn't share his experiences when the others did. He would moan when we started a new exercise. He really didn't want to be there. This was all a bunch of hogwash.

Guess who had the strongest reaction of all? John. He reported that he went home that night and sat on the bed. He didn't remember going to sleep or into meditation, but he did remember that a huge snake rose up from the base of his spine. He was instantly taken to a place that he described as pure bliss, with scintillating lights and light beings cheering him on as he knelt before God. God touched him and told him he was proud of him. Needless to say, John has never been the same since. His life was transformed. He is now a believer.

Alan and Joanne's Story

This couple came to one of the kundalini workshops. Alan ran the relationship and Joanne was a "yes" person. She did whatever he asked. As part of the workshop, everyone broke into groups to talk about the theme issues they were working through in this and past lifetimes. Alan and Joanne joined the same group. The theme was masculine-feminine imbalance. It wasn't long before I heard a heated discussion in that group and moved closer to listen. Joanne was saying to Alan, "You are a big baby. I always give to you first. I'm not going to do that anymore. It is my turn now." She meant what she said. She said it from a position of power. Now, the whole dynamic of that relationship has changed due to the transformative kundalini energy. They are now both equally powerful in a healthy and loving partnership.

DUANE'S STORY

Duane was injured as a child and had irreparable brain damage. The doctors said he was a hopeless case and would never have motor-skill control. Duane has been in several of my kundalini workshops. Despite the brain damage, he is now speaking more fluidly and his comprehension level is much higher. It turns out that he is brilliant technically and spiritually, and he is able to verbally share his wisdom with others. Either the kundalini rewired his brain, or his mind has taken over and is working around the damaged areas. What a gift!

I hope that sharing these stories helps you see that kundalini affects all aspects of our lives: physical, mental, emotional, psychological, and spiritual. More than half the people who have taken these kundalini workshops are experiencing life more intuitively and they see auras.

KUNDALINI EXERCISES

These exercises will enhance the flow of your kundalini. If you do these exercises, please use moderation. They are safe; but if you feel too much energy, please use common sense and stop before you hurt yourself. If you hurt yourself, it will take time to heal and the intense effort will be for nothing because you'll have to start all over. Remember, your body is a beautiful temple to be treated sweetly and tenderly.

Guided Imagery

Close your eyes and imagine that you are sitting in the middle of a pond on a lily pad. The lily pad is white and has many petals. The fragrance is so fresh and clear that it opens up your senses. As you breathe in this fragrance, imagine that you are sitting in the lotus position with your eyes closed. As you breathe in and out, say "OM." As you inhale, say "OM." As you exhale, say "OM."

You may begin to feel a vibration inside your body. As the vibration becomes stronger, you may feel an expansion inside as the sound of "OM" resonates. Really feel your body. Expand with the vibration and invite the kundalini by saying something like, "Goddess Kundalini, I honor you. Please let your presence be felt." Become aware of any sensations you may have inside or around you. Sit for a few more moments and notice how you feel, perhaps more peaceful and centered. Thank Goddess Kundalini, or the kundalini force, for coming, even if you didn't feel anything.

Repetition is very important in doing these practices. Use this exercise to release stress, or just to feel good. If you are in a public place and can't chant out loud, sing under your breath. It works just the same.

Kundalini Exercise One

Lie on your back with hands beside you and the palms down. Use your heels to move your body. Rock back and forth from head to feet. Do this twenty times. Then lie still for a minute or so. Then hold your head as you slowly sit up. You've been raising spinal fluid. You may feel a swelling sensation across your sacrum.

Kundalini Exercise Two

Lie on your back with knees up and hands on the floor beside you. Start moving your breath up and down your spine. On the inhale, breathe air in from the top of your head down to the base of the spine. On the exhale, breathe back up from the base of the spine and out the top of your head. Repeat several times until you feel the need to breathe normally. Lie still and feel your body. Then hold your head with your hand as you sit up.

Kundalini Exercise Three

This exercise is called the "Breath of Fire." Sit with your back erect, close your eyes, and put your hands in a comfortable position on your knees or in your lap. Begin breathing rapidly in and out through your nose, using your solar plexus as a pump. If you have trouble with this, you can place your hand on the solar plexus so you can feel the breath moving in and out. As you do this, place emphasis on the exhale.

Breathe in and out twenty to fifty times, then sit still for a few minutes. Notice how still your mind is. If it isn't still, breathe some more.

Then notice if there is pain or pressure anywhere in your body. If there is, breathe through those areas. Imagine that you are breathing the pain or congestion out of your body.

If you want to give this energy to someone else, you can do so. Alternate breathing and resting for about ten minutes. Then stand behind the person, place your hands on the head, and breath energy down through your own arms and hands into the person. He/she will probably feel heat. If you do this long enough, he/she will experience peace, love, and healing.

Kundalini

NINE

Ascension

The topic of ascension is very popular now. Everybody wants to know where he/she is on the grand scale of measuring light. Most are thinking, "Surely I've paid enough dues (karma) by now and I'm ready for the great rewards in Heaven." We are in the new millennium, and the new age is here. We have an extraordinary opportunity right now to become who we really are at our source. Godliness is our innate quality and we're becoming that again. This is really an exciting time to be on the planet.

The truth is, the planet herself is in her enlightenment process. Vibrationally, Earth is rising in frequency all the time in her ascension back into the Godhead. As the entire universe grows and expands, all bodies of light (you and me) expand and grow also. Earth's vibration has been three-dimensional and very dense for a long time. Now Earth's aura is opening, and the more she expands into the more subtle (light) levels, such as the fourth and fifth dimensions, the more light we become. I like the fact that the entire creation is expanding and I am a part of the process. That is so exciting!

We chose to be here on this planet at this time. We signed on the dotted line and said, "I'll go now. I'll be there at the beginning of the new millennium, and I'll serve wherever and however I am supposed to, to fulfill my mission." All of us are gifted in many areas that will serve God and the masses. Some people are adept at survival strategies or midwifery or cooking or finding water. Others are drawn to organizing finances or building structures. The list goes on. It is not by accident that you have incarnated at this time, wanting to ascend. Your area of expertise will be utilized when you are called upon to serve.

In some religions and philosophies, service is called seva (service to God). There is no faster way to burn off karma than to practice your spiritual disciplines, and the one at the top of the list is seva.

There are many areas of service. It can involve starting meetings, setting-up and cleaning-up afterwards, volunteering at church, delivering food to elderly people on holidays, cooking and cleaning for a neighbor who is ill, or offering some service free to the community (whatever your community is, neighborhood, church, or organization).

The 1990s, the last decade before the millennium change, were about self-exploration and examination. That is why there are so many counselors, therapists, psychics, and healers available now. Not only do more people want their work to be in a holistic alternative area, many also want to have more than one area of expertise, such as hands-on healing and counseling. To make a long story short, we are in a Golden Age and this age is so very rich with many service-oriented jobs so we can both serve others and make a living.

The field of therapy is shifting rapidly now and that is concerning a lot of traditional mental health practitioners and organizations. Some practitioners are outgrowing the traditional system in a revolutionary way. Many of the new techniques and practices now being used are unknown to the Psychological Board. This is because many of us are doing what is called "brief therapy," which means just that, "brief." We are in a hurry to get the old negative blocks out of the body, aura, mind, nervous system, and personality. We want to be light enough to ascend. This means we are all working diligently to get rid of mass; this includes outlived habits, thoughts, and behaviors as well as negative feelings about ourselves and others. We want God-consciousness. And that is what the new millennium is all about: getting in touch with what is on board, taking inventory of what is outdated, and eliminating what doesn't serve us well anymore.

As high-minded people, we want to move into a peaceful place where we are not controlled by our own shadow (or dark) side, or anyone else's. This means we are leaning toward practical means of becoming whole. This involves a lot of self-examination and monitoring of our intention (i.e., Do I have a hidden agenda in this good deed I'm performing?)

Selfless giving must come from a pure intent and a pure heart. Because there is so much illusion, we think we are giving selflessly, but are we really? Sometimes we need to stop and ask ourselves if there is a personal pay-off from our good deeds, or if we are truly clear and loving in our intent. I have tested myself on this several times over the last few years. I have given to someone secretly, then waited to see if I could keep it to myself. And I listened to my inner dialogue to see if my ego grabbed hold of the good deed and claimed it as its own, or if I gave truly from the heart.

Unconditional love is the big leap in the ascension

process. I believe we really haven't gotten deeply into the ascension process until we are unconditionally loving most of the time. Even if we are not able to adhere to the values and rules that go along with this state of being, I think we should be conscious of it at all times and weigh each act to determine whether it is unconditional or not.

In *Power vs. Force*, David R. Hawkins, M.D. measures each feeling or behavior in "light degrees" (megahertz). Obviously the lower emotions or states weigh heavier and are lower on the scale. Unconditional love measures 500, joy at 540, peace and bliss at 600, and enlightenment at 700-1000. We have to overcome many obstacles to become unconditionally loving and giving. It is worth it. Unfortunately, most of the human race measures in the 200 to 300 range. But if enough of us are vibrating at least 450 to 500, we can lift the consciousness of all humanity and the planet and aid in the process at a global level.

In kundalini workshops, I measure the groups' vibration level by using kinesiology in the beginning to see where we all calibrate as a group, then again at the end of the workshop. We are always surprised by how many points the group has gone up after doing all the spiritual exercises and meditations. Then, of course, as a group the vibration is compounded. We consciously send our love out to all countries, to all the peoples, and to the planet herself. I guess the whole point in desiring the ascension process-the going home-is to be able to help others, serve in any way we can, and remain open to whatever God has in mind for us.

I feel peaceful when I am functioning from my higher self. I know I am being maneuvered and moved exactly where I should be going. I trust completely when I am being moved or quieted by spirit. I also know when I am out of sync and my thought processes include jealously, sloth, greed, envy, worry, anger, laziness, and/or smallness of mind; or when the ego tries to convince me there isn't enough to go around. Sometimes I get locked into a fear and, even though at a higher conscious level I know it's going to be "all right," I flounder around in the emotions of the lower chakras. I know then that another layer of the same old theme has come to the surface for me to clear in order to reach peace again. The lower body systems and chakras hold the lower feelings and desires that make us feel insecure.

When I find myself in these mental places, I sit down and ask, "What's going on with me? What am I afraid of? How do I feel threatened?" Then I look at the worst possible scenario and realize that the worst really isn't so bad after all. I then go back to God, most of the time laughing at the absurdity of my small thoughts and feelings.

Many times, when I read something on ascension, I chuckle because I know that all people have been ascended masters in past lives. We've already done this drama before. And those of us who have awakened spiritually and consciously are seeking sainthood again in this lifetime. It has been billions of years since we left the great cosmic God, and now we're headed back up into the Godhead. As we do ascend, we realize that we never really left.

What about those strands of DNA-our unique identity? They've always been our connection to God. They come down from spirit and into the body, and more and more strands are activated as we expand in our enlightenment.

In my own personal experience I find that daily meditation is helpful and keeps me connected to the Lord within. I also chant the name of God daily. And I have an ongoing conversation with my inner God. I personally pray to God. But it matters not who your God is-Jesus, Krishna,

Rama, Buddha, Allah, Jehovah, Whoever. I ask God what I should do when I am in turmoil, or I imagine what He/She/It would do given the same circumstances.

At one point in my ascension process, I was overshadowed by my spiritual saint. This overshadowing was actually witnessed by a third party who visually watched as the saint's form dropped into my body. The witness described the facial features of the saint and watched the process until I was fully embodied by this being. Once I became aware of what was happening, I was able to witness it myself when looking into a mirror.

Another thing I find helpful when I become self-absorbed and caught up in the drama of life is to find someone else to help. It's like magic. In helping others, we are given grace by God. God takes care of all our needs. We immediately forget our own problems when helping someone else.

These have been some practical exercises to do when you are caught up in yourself and the drama of everyday life. If you do them, you'll become more peaceful and closer to God each day. If you forget all these things, then just breathe and say, "God" as you inhale, and "God" or "OM" as you exhale.

Another exercise that is helpful is the following guided-imagery. As you infuse energy into this imagined scene and give it power and action, you will be creating balance, happiness, and health for yourself and the entire planet with all of her people. What a gift to humankind, what an unconditionally loving gift of service.

GUIDED IMAGERY

Close your eyes, take three deep breaths, and imagine that you are viewing everything from above as if you are in a satellite. You can see all the different countries. Imagine all the people, some rich and some with just barely enough food, water, and shelter.

A loving thing to imagine is dropping down into the people who have more than enough and talking to them from your heart. Ask them to donate to the less fortunate people, and imagine that they are agreeing to give. Imagine yourself delivering goods to the less fortunate, and feel passion as you give to them. Know that the joy you feel is not for yourself, but for the people receiving this love. Also feel appreciation and respect for the wealthy people who were generous enough to be willing to share.

You can make this a daily discipline or ritual and choose a different country each time. Don't forget the U.S.A.

As a result of training your mind to give and to be an ambassador of giving, you and your perceptions will expand and soon you will find yourself looking for good things to do for others. Of course, the rewards are ten-fold. But that's not why you are giving. You are giving because you are beginning the process of creating and manifesting. The more you visualize or imagine good and fair things happening to others, the more you will become one of the people who is making a difference on this planet. Maybe you will be instrumental in creating world peace. I think it will happen this way.

LIGHTBODY

As part of the ascension process, there are energetic changes that take place within the aura and body that enable us to rise in vibration and connect more consciously with our soul and spirit. (Within the higher self, the soul is the level below the spirit. The level above spirit is the godhead.) A central part of the ascension process is the development of a lightbody which, in essence, is a grid of light that forms around our body to connect each cell of the physical body to our spirit and to the Divine. In other words, as you form your lightbody, you are connecting Heaven and Earth and merging your higher and lower selves.

The process begins with developing a grid of light similar to a spider web that connects you to your soul. Through this grid your soul can send sound and light in the appropriate frequency or color to rewire your physical structure. This will enable you to handle the higher vibration and new information you will be receiving.

This process truly is enlightenment (en-LIGHTenment)! Within the physical body this entails reprogramming and cleansing all of the body systems including vascular, lymph, endocrine, and nervous systems. Rewiring also takes place in the brain as new pathways open up and dormant sections and glands activate. Prior to the formation of the lightbody, the energy that fueled the body was biological. Part of the physical transformation of this process is that the cells begin to recognize light as an additional energy source.

Also part of this process is the connecting of new strands of DNA. As learned in high school, humans now have only two active strands of DNA. This limits our abilities and our reality. Most importantly, it keeps us in a three-dimensional reality and disconnects us from receiving messages from the higher self. As part of the ascension process, additional strands hook in. Most sources say that we acquire one new DNA stand per initiation (see "Initiations" below). For example, the third strand becomes connected to the body as part of the Third Initiation, or "Soul Merge."

Part of this structural metamorphosis is the need to clear away blockages and other limitations within the body.

These include unresolved emotional issues, limiting beliefs, and disease. One form that these blockages can take is "crystals" that healers or clairvoyants can see or feel in the body and aura. The additional light that the soul sends through the grid increases the rate of cellular metabolism which forces lower vibrational blocks such as toxins, memories, and traumas to be released. Many of the healing techniques in this book are helpful for facilitating this transformation. You will probably find yourself drawn to various forms of bodywork, therapy (e.g., psychotherapy or hypnotherapy), and dietary changes as you move through this process.

The higher your vibration becomes, the more connected to spirit you are and the more you open to perceiving other dimensions and higher knowledge. We live in the third dimension. In expansion, you move out of the third dimension and into the fourth dimension where good and bad karma are held. This gives you the opportunity to clear these unresolved issues and agreements. As you continue to expand, you are able to perceive more dimensions and you gain access to the angelic kingdom, ascended masters, creators and co-creators, and the geometric light forms such as the "circle" which is the blueprint for creation. As you change, so does all of creation. Each change affects the entire system.

I am able to watch the development of the lightbody in my clients. It starts forming around the head and shoulders and heart area. Then it works its way through the rest of the body and aura. It comes from above and works its way down. The spirit drops the light down in. It also drops in liquid protein through the lines of light. Spirit starts the grid in the spine as well. So then you have not only the light from above coming in from spirit, but also the spine is building the grid. You have it coming from the inside and from the outside. I also have witnessed angels and fairies and other spiritual beings actually working within the grid to connect the lines. I refer to them as spiritual "silk worms."

Unified Chakra

As part of the lightbody development, additional higher chakras become activated. The number and location of these additional chakras varies from author to author, but typically seven additional chakras are described. Eventually these additional chakras and the seven physical body chakras open and merge into a "unified chakra." Prior to this opening, the physical body chakras are cone-shaped in the front and back of the body (second through sixth chakras), above the top of the head (seventh), and below the base of the spine (first). This cone shape is caused by an energy blockage in the center along the spine. Sometime after the Fourth Initiation-renunciation of attachment to people, places, things-the seals begin to break and the cone-shaped chakras expand to spherical shape. As they continue to expand, they eventually merge with each other and the seven higher chakras to form one "unified chakra" centered at the heart.

As a clairvoyant watching this process, I have noted that after the seal along the spine breaks, the chakra shifts and expands into an irregular elliptical movement that ultimately becomes spherical. I have also noticed that the process varies from person to person. In at least one case, the shift was instantaneous with all chakras opening and unifying at once. This occurrence was so powerful that I felt the ripple effect of the energy in myself for several weeks after the initiation ceremony. In most people the process is gradual, with the individual chakras opening as the chakra-specific issues are resolved. It also happens that the front (or back) of one chakra can open and become elliptical while the other side remains cone-shaped.

There are many symptoms or side-effects that most people experience while undergoing the development of their lightbody and the unified chakra. This is a huge transformation process. After all, we are talking here about changing the genetic structure of the physical body and opening to an entirely new way of creating our reality. Physical symptoms can include looking younger; changes in body size and shape, including an enlarged head as brain changes occur; body pain; and hormone level fluctuations that can produce symptoms similar to pregnancy or menopause. Psychological changes can include moving out of denial and facing your issues; moving beyond caring what other people think; having lucid dreams or visions of past lives; feeling like you are going crazy; and developing intuitive gifts.

An interesting way to view the changes in the aura during the ascension process is via Kirlian photography (aura photographs). The Kirlian photographer uses a specially designed camera that records not only the image of the physical body, but also the colors of the aura. These aura photographs are usually available at psychic fairs or metaphysical expositions. They usually cost about twenty dollars and include a psychic reading of the aura by the photographer. A reading usually includes the significance of the various colors that appear, the shape and size of the aura, and any issues perceived. Anything visible on the right side of the body is something that is leaving; anything on the left side represents something moving in; anything in the middle or above the head indicates the present. Many times guides are visible standing around the body in the aura. Through the years I have had regular Kirlian photos taken and now have a series of ten or twelve photos that show the changes in my aura and my spiritual growth through the past fifteen years. In the beginning my aura did not show a lot of light. Gradually in my enlightenment process the aura holds more light every year. Since 1996 my aura seems to change every four to six months. It is interesting to see the progression from one picture to the next due to the change in color, resilience, and vibrancy. Each color vibrates differently from dense to light. The photos have helped me identify some issues I needed to clear. Next time a psychic fair is in your town, go have an aura photo taken.

For more detailed information on the forming of the lightbody, there are many books available. Two good books about the lightbody and unified chakra are *What is Lightbody?* in which Tashira Tachi-ren channels the Archangel Ariel, and *The Ascension Handbook* in which Tony Stubbs channels Serapis. Other related materials on ascension or enlightenment include *Dark Night of the Soul* by St. John of the Cross, *Play of Consciousness* by Baba Muktananda, *My Lord Loves a Pure Heart* by Gurumayi, and *The Book of Knowledge: The Keys of Enoch* by J. J. Hurtak.

INITIATIONS AND THE ENLIGHTENMENT PROCESS

There are as many different belief systems on the topic of ascension and enlightenment as there are people. A review of all the religions or lineages shows us that everything we read or hear today is essentially all the same message. This is true whether it is eastern philosophy, the Alice Bailey works (Great White Brotherhood), or the Bible. I'm going to give some mental information on our history from the beginning. It's called cosmology, the study of the cosmos.

And in the beginning there was light. Billions of years ago we left God as spirits and started the involutionary process, the coming into matter. This is called the Cosmic Day, or the coming out of God as spirit. At last we have finished this process after living thousands, even millions, of lives in over a four-billion-year time period. It is very likely we have been everything from a ballet dancer to a thief, a murderer to a saint. We have done all of this and more. The more light we house, the more enlightened we become. This means we must release the nonpositive or dense matter within our four-body system (physical, mental, emotional, spiritual). Density is the false beliefs and old habits or lies about who we are. In other words, you came into this life as an ascended master and now are reading this material because it is time to remember and comprehensively understand this. If you were not at a high level of awareness, this information would be of no interest to you and would be too complex to understand.

My favorite explanations of the ascension process come through the Alice Bailey works, St. John of the Cross, and the Eastern Indian lineages and its saints. During my years of experience facilitating the enlightenment process in my clients, I have worked most closely with the Alice Bailey/Djwhal Kuhl system. Alice Bailey channeled Djwhal Kuhl, an ascended master. He says there are six initiations and a portion of a seventh that can be completed on planet Earth as we raise our light vibration up to the highest level possible. There are further initiations that are done on the other side.

This system, which was introduced in the 1930s, seems, in my opinion, to have been somewhat modified or superceded during these current times of accelerated energies and spiritual expansion. This expansion includes not only humans, but the planet herself and all the kingdoms. It is my sense that it is now possible to undergo further initiations and illumination while still in the body. Most recently, I resonate more with St. John of the Cross. He identifies nine steps that can be done in the body while living on planet Earth. The tenth step is "God-absorption," when we (in most people) cease to be in a physical body.

The following information is my own interpretation of the spiritual stages and initiations we go through in the enlightenment process. It is a blend of these other explanations, plus my own observations and experience as a facilitator. I have helped literally hundreds of people prepare for initiations. As I become a conduit, I am used by the masters to conduct the initiation ceremonies, and transfer the light to the initiates. And I help with the integration process. Each initiation is a process and has several levels that must be integrated before proceeding to the next initiation. This integration process can take months or years or lifetimes, depending on the individual. Many people are in the enlightenment process and are not even aware of it. I can intuitively see the indicators in their auras.

The timing of initiations is determined by favorable conditions in the solar system and in the individual's astrological chart. However, I have helped facilitate initiations that were not astrologically favorable. This was a forced (early) initiation, but not harmful. This is possible if the initiation is aided by a full moon and/or if the initiate's aura contains enough light and is resilient enough to handle the intense downpour of light from above.

FIRST AND SECOND INITIATIONS

First Initiation. The First Initiation is physical survival. We began as Neanderthals learning to survive. And we mastered that one. So that took us to the Second Initiation.

Second Initiation. This is the emotional awakening. Our feeling centers (chakras) open up. This involves having feelings and love for others and self; and having appreciation for beautiful things and sensual manifestations such as light, color, and comfort. After accepting and appreciating our emotional self, we move onto the Third Initiation which is the first spiritual initiation.

THIRD INITIATION, THE BEGINNING OF SOUL MERGE

The Third Initiation is a pivotal point in our spiritual enlightenment process. At this point, the soul anchors into the physical body. Since birth we have been functioning with a limited amount of soul-essence in our being. Now we begin to overcome the lower aspects of self and become aware that there is a greater portion of soul we have not yet embodied, called the oversoul. The oversoul is part of the higher self.

In the Third Initiation, you begin the process of connecting to, or merging with, your oversoul. During the initiation ceremony a portion of the soul comes into your body. The majority continues to reside on the spiritual plane as the oversoul. Throughout the integration of this initiation, the oversoul continues to drop more and more of its light and characteristics into you. The rate that this happens varies from person to person, depending upon the plan of your oversoul. The more intensely and persistently you clear your issues, the more "soul light" your body can house. If you are too eager, then your cup runneth over and some of the light is temporarily lost.

During integration of this initiation, you learn to use your mental body. It is at this point that you begin to comprehend who you are and where you fit into the scheme of All That Is. Your search for God becomes persistent. You want to feel the presence of God in your life. At this stage it is helpful to do at least one spiritual discipline (e.g., meditation, chanting, prayer, yoga) each day to strengthen your contact with God.

You are in the probationary process. Your spiritual masters take you on as a disciple. They watch and help you in your expansion and upward spiral. Unfortunately, your intuitive gifts may not develop until the end of this stage or later, so it sometimes is difficult to trust that you are being guided. You may question whether this is even real.

You can go through grief as the negative ego-self begins to die because the changes create an identity crisis. At this point you may feel very confused and uninvolved with everyday life, including relationships. You no longer relate to the world and your life as you did previously. You may begin to feel you are less than other people because you feel that your service to God is not enough. Despite your hard work to become one with God, you usually perceive few rewards because you are not satisfied by worldly things as much and all of your efforts can seem small. As your heart begins to open, you may feel overwhelmed by your feeling of love for all things and excited to have a purpose now.

This also can be a very lonely time. You sometimes may feel lost between the physical self and the spiritual Self. You may feel worthless and empty. Unfortunately, some people react to this loneliness by placing too much value on a relationship with a mate. If the mate is not on the same spiritual path, your emotional clearing and spiritual growth may be stunted because you may drop to his/her level to be compatible, and your focus is on the relationship rather than your enlightenment. You may also quit practicing the spiritual disciplines that were moving you along. On the other hand, your mate can be stimulated by your enlightenment process and begin his/her own ascension.

This is an important phase of the initiation process, and it is a time when you need to do a lot of clearing and purging of false beliefs. This purification is necessary so you can be clear enough to house more and more of your oversoul. The kundalini is stimulated and begins burning within. It burns out old habits and negativity. If you are working diligently to clear your negativity, your vanity and judgment of self and others will begin to dissipate as you become clearer.

In my work with facilitating initiations, I know that someone is ready for the Third Initiation (Soul Merge) by the size of his/her "soul star" and *antahkarana*. The soul star is a body of light located above the head. The *antahkarana*, as defined in many spiritual works such as "The Alice Bailey Works," is the divine shaft of light that moves through you, extending from above the head to below the feet, connecting you to both Heaven and Earth. It varies in size from the size of a quarter to very wide, depending on your level of awareness.

People who are not ready for Soul Merge generally have an *antahkarana* about the size of a quarter. Some are only the size of a string. The more that the soul drops light down into the body via the *antahkarana*, the more the *antahkarana* opens. The larger the *antahkarana*, the more the soul star can drop down. Someone who is ready to prepare for Soul Merge has an *antahkarana* about the size of a cantaloupe. Once he/she has done enough clearing to prepare for the initiation, it is usually about the size of a basketball, and the soul star is a ball of light two to three feet in diameter.

Soul merge can happen naturally without any conscious preparation or a facilitated ceremony. However, in this case the *antahkarana* widens to the point that it is larger than the body and the soul just drops in. After a person's

Soul Merge, I can see the light of the soul in the aura. Also, the grid of the lightbody begins to build, usually around the throat and head. At this point, the soul star is no longer visible above the head, because during the initiation this part of the soul drops into the heart. This initiation begins the opening of the heart.

PATRISHA'S PRE-SOUL-MERGE EXPERIENCE

About twenty-five years ago I had what was essentially a meeting with my oversoul. I was lying down, preparing to die because life was so painful. I thought I could do just that. I was putting my life in the hands of Christ and expecting I would be taken. Instead, I suddenly felt myself filled from head to toe with light that was very tangible and profound. I jumped up, joyfully crying, and knew I had a mission on this planet. I was filled with bliss. This experience gave me a preview of what was to come years later when I soul-merged into the hands of God.

PATRISHA'S SOUL-MERGE EXPERIENCE

In 1985 I attended a soul-merge weekend of ten people. Only two people actually soul-merged. I was not one of them. My ego was crushed. I immediately and fervently began seeing every channel and healer I could find to clear me. But this was to no avail. I was trying too hard. What I know now, but did not know then, is that all initiations happen at the appropriate time, and not before. The timing is determined by spirit, not ego.

My soul-merge experience happened spontaneously in the middle of the night. I awoke and saw light everywhere. I jumped out of bed thinking there was a UFO outside my window. I looked out, but there was no UFO. Instead, when I turned around, the light was in the room and in my body. The soul (oversoul) could not get into my body until I was asleep and beyond the control of my conscious mind and ego!

I went before God and He/She/It touched me on both shoulders with the "Rod of Power." My masters were there: Djwahl Kuhl, Vywamus, St. Germaine, and Kwan Yin. They were masters I was familiar with from my reading and studies. Also present were a host of angels and old friends from past lives, all celebrating this important event. Light exploded everywhere as if fireworks were going off. A choir was singing. The message from God to me was that I had never been disconnected from Him/Her/It. I had always been loved and always would be. My mission was-and is-to help lift the light vibration of humans and our planet Earth.

This experience was emotionally moving. My heart opened and I experienced unconditional love. I wept with joy, in remembrance of my place in Heaven. I went back often to this place to be replenished and filled again with love and light. Now, I am able to go to an even higher place.

Facilitating a Soul-Merge Initiation

The facilitation process is an intuitive one. It is very rewarding because of the amount of light that pours down from above. My preference is to begin with the initiate sitting in a chair. I use different techniques to clear away any blockages or barricades, false beliefs or fears. Sometimes, we simply talk about the issue. Sometimes, I use techniques such as those described in chapter five. Many times we need to clear a failed attempt in a past life by using a past-life regression technique from chapter four. After the majority of false beliefs and patterns have been removed, the initiate then moves to a massage table. Etheric or new age music is played softly in the background to set the mood. Candles, essential oils, or anything else spiritual and gentle may be used. The initiate lies face up on the table.

As a healer, you may want to scan the aura and clear away any nonpositive debris so the initiate's soul can slip in easier. If there are hot spots on the body, this means there is congestion in that area, so it is appropriate to clear the heat or any other physical obstacles that might be present.

As soon as the body is clear you begin an expansion process. During this process, the emotional and mental body leave the physical body and expand to become incredibly large, as large as the universe. This allows the initiate to be able to go to the place where God resides, whatever that may be for the person. The process of expansion takes about twenty minutes and you will have the initiate expand in stages, first as large as the building, then as large as the city block, then as large as the city, then the state, then the country, and then the planet. After each expansion, have the initiate integrate that level. The initiate should be experiencing the feeling of floating or levitating. Have the initiate imagine that he/she is floating over the planet and that the planet is inside the aura. Finally, have the initiate expand until he/she is as large as the universe and the universe is inside the initiate.

As soon as the initiate is part of the universe, ask him/her to take a look around or feel the surroundings. The initiate may experience comets going through the self, planets spinning within the self. Have the initiate sensually feel these things so he/she is completely absorbed in the process. Never let the initiate start laughing or making light of this process, because that is the ego trying to stop the process; things have gotten too big and the ego is losing control. Take your time with the initiate and make sure he/she is sensually involved in the process-feeling heat, feeling love and peace, filling up with light, and experiencing bliss.

As soon as you feel the initiate is acclimated and one hundred percent into the initiation, ask him/her to look around and imagine a bright light. Most of the time, the initiate is able to see it. However, if not, help the initiate fly around the universe until he/she finds the light by either seeing it or feeling it. Go with the initiate. As soon as the initiate is in the presence of the light, have him/her move right into it and be absorbed by it. Nine times out of ten, when you ask the initiate what is being experienced, he/she will say, "Light. Just light. Blinding light."

The initiate is to stay in this light until he/she becomes fully absorbed in it and can now see beyond the light. Tell the initiate to look around to see if there are any beings, masters or angels. Have the initiate describe who is there. If the initiate is not able to see any beings, have him/her call forth masters and angels, and they will come. The beings that will be there will be the initiate's own guiding masters who have shown up for the initiation celebration.

Have the initiate ask these beings if they have come to take him/her somewhere. Have the initiate extend a hand so the master can lead. Fly along with the initiate as he/she is being led to the initiation place. The initiate may be seeing columns, steps, marble floors, an altar, anything. He/she may go on a shamanic journey, or may even be under the sea with dolphins or whales. Have the initiate describe what is being seen and felt. That way you aren't programming him/her. The initiation will be whatever the person needs to experience, and this will vary depending on the initiate's belief system. As soon as the initiate arrives at the initiation site, ask him/her to look around to see who is there. There are usually three masters standing around the initiate. The masters are there to receive and modify the light from God. The masters give this light to the initiate as he/she is ready to receive it.

Usually there are groups of people at the ceremony who have come to celebrate and welcome the initiate into Heaven. This is the real beginning of the ascension process. At some point, God appears, usually as a Golden Being, and may hold the initiate lovingly or touch him/her with a Divine Rod of Light. Have the initiate ask God if there is a message. There may or may not be. Once this person has been either touched, spoken to, or is in the presence of God, this is the point when the soul merges with the emotional and mental bodies. There may be a celebration. Beings may surround the initiate. Or there could be choirs singing. If the initiate is not visually seeing much, you can describe what you are seeing or experiencing. However, only do this if you are sure the person cannot see on his/her own. It is best if the initiate experiences this personally.

At some point, the initiate will experience a profound sense of peace. This is the one thing that always happens, no matter what else the experience may include. Ask the initiate to enjoy that moment of peace. It is profound. And ask him/her to bring this peace back when returning to the physical body. Just quietly stand beside the initiate. As soon as he/she has absorbed the peace, the initiate immediately will be back in the body. Ask the initiate to say when he/she has returned.

Tape the ceremony so the initiate has the Soul Merge experience on tape. Listening to this tape is especially helpful to the initiate when the ego is trying to tell him/her it didn't really happen. If there are any afterthoughts, these should go on the tape as well. Congratulate the initiate and tell him/her that during the probationary period, he/she will be watched over day and night by the masters; they will be there as a support system to guide and protect the initiate and make sure the power of the soul is not misused.

You can tell the initiate some of the symptoms that may happen during the integration of the initiation; these can include hot flashes that can cause sleeping difficulty. The initiate can always ask for this heat to be modified or cooled down. Sometimes there are gaps in the memory because soul is pulling out masses of old thought-forms and there is a temporary hole in the mind. The initiate may start experiencing creative aspects of self. A female may feel pregnant and temporarily gain about ten pounds of weight because the body knows there is something new within it and may assume it is pregnant. There may be moments of bliss and ecstasy, or even spontaneous crying from joy and love. These are the moments when the soul is present in the body. It comes in and out during the integration period. The soul (oversoul) drops down through the *antahkarana* and drops a tremendous amount of light into the body to be integrated at the body's own speed. Then it pulls back up again.

If the initiate wants to speed up the process of the Soul Merge, he/she can memorize the Soul Mantra and say it several times a day:
 I am the soul.
 I am the light divine.
 I am love.
 I am divine will.
 I am fixed and perfect design.
 I am aligned.

Integration of the Third Initiation varies with each person. Quick is one year. Slow can take the rest of your life. However, due to the accelerated energies today, the initiations are integrating much faster with some people. A good book that can be read in preparation for Soul Merge is

The Rainbow Bridge, Phase II, Link with the Soul, written by Two Disciples.

FOURTH INITIATION

In this initiation you continue to embody more and more soul. Divine spirit, or I AM Presence, also becomes active through the soul in this stage. Strands of light drop down at this time. Spirit is the portion of your higher self that is an ocean of light above and beyond the oversoul. The spirit contains the blueprint for our perfect Self that ultimately will be embodied at the culmination of your enlightenment process on Earth. Its energy is so cosmically electric that at this point you really can't embody much, if any, of the spirit. Therefore, the soul must serve as a buffer between it and you.

The prerequisites for this initiation, which happen during the integration of the Third Initiation, include the initial stages of purification; the beginning of detachment to all people, places, and things; and learning to take responsibility for your own creations. Once you are in the initiation process, your "victim consciousness" begins to break down.

Also in the Fourth Initiation, you gain access to High Mind, High Intuition, and High Will (spiritual power). You become more powerful and must be careful not to misuse these higher abilities. Usually these powers are given only as you clear enough of the lower nature to use them wisely and with love. In this initiation, you also begin to see the divine plan. You are then able to see the bigger picture. You get the "ah ha's!" and begin to understand what is really going on. You are also able to comprehend spiritual principles such as service to God and humankind. In the face of these principles, by the end of this stage you become less interested in your own self-interest and dramas.

Your heart opens further and you begin to feel things deeply. This cannot happen until you begin to be emotionally detached and divinely indifferent. Otherwise you would not be able to tolerate the pain, yours and everyone else's. In order for the heart opening to continue, you must be purified of your lower chakra issues. This is why Alice Bailey/Djwhal Kuhl refer to the Fourth Initiation as the initiation of renunciation. The major work of this initiation is to release your attachments to people, places, and things: money, power, jobs, success, family, and any desire-level addictions. This can be a very painful process. Despite the fact that financial issues and losses can be part of the releasing of attachments, God always takes care of our survival needs. God gives us love through our spirit, but this can be confusing because it is given internally and we are not always able to perceive it. You do have moments of God's love and joy periodically, but much of the time you may feel very separated. You must therefore become consciously aware of what has been removed or transformed so you can be encouraged by your growth as a result of your efforts. You must continue on with trust and faith as the divine "carrot" is dangled in front of you to keep you going.

This is a stage of impatience because you have become hungry for enlightenment. You have a vision of spirit but are unable to embody it due to your residual unresolved ego-level issues. The breaking down of the layers of the ego is part of this process. In fact, you enter a stage referred to as the "Dark Night of the Soul." I believe this is the stage where Jesus "was tested" by God by being sent into the desert to be tempted with the lower desires of his shadow side. During the Dark Night, God symbolically takes you into the desert and strips you clean of your old nonpositive behaviors and patterns. The identity of the ego-personality is erased, layer by layer. During this period, you may experience loneliness and despair and feel like you are totally alone and abandoned by God. You may feel like you have no direction, don't know where to go, how to act, what to do, or even how to be.

Although some people don't experience this, during my Dark Night I felt totally and completely alone for a two-year period. I would make plans with people, but forget the plans I had made and spend my days and nights alone. Memory lapses were common because the oversoul periodically removed masses of negative thought-forms, leaving an empty space in my aura. Soon the aura would re-coagulate and my memory would be restored. I cried a lot and prayed to God for this phase to pass quickly. I also meditated much of the time, but my pain was so deep that I felt like the meditations were unfruitful. As I awakened more and more consciously to my past behaviors, I was filled with remorse and shame. Once, driving in the mountains, I wondered what it would be like to drive off the cliff. Thoughts of suicide were common, but I always remembered my son. Also during the Dark Night, my shadow side became very obvious. As I searched desperately for an escape from the pain, I found myself tempted to revisit all of my old addictive behaviors such as alcohol, drugs, gambling, sex, shopping, and bingeing on sugar. I settled for the lesser of these evils and maxed several credit cards and single-handedly supported the ice cream industry. The fact that I did not drive off the cliff, nor resume the most destructive addictive behaviors, is evidence to me of how, no matter how alone and abandoned we feel, God is there guiding and protecting us.

This is a stage of hard work and of feeling blinded and disconnected from God and all things. You can undergo habitual suffering, but whether you realize it or not you are given enough energy by God to keep you on your upward path. Nevertheless, you may still feel cut off from God because you still identify with your ego or human self. You have not expanded high enough, nor embodied enough light to identify totally with your oversoul and spirit. As you continue to clear your issues and grow spiritually, many of your friends and family members may have difficulty understanding you. Your consciousness steadily expands. Your interests become different. Some of these people move out of your life. This can be very painful and lonely. Eventually you do develop new friends, and the relationships within your family change. You are more compassionate regarding other people's problems. But you can become so discouraged that you give up and stop asking even God for help. You don't even know what to ask for, because life has become so unpredictable.

By the end of the Fourth Initiation, as you approach the Fifth Initiation, you move into a better space. You are able to feel God's gift of love and joy. You become more detached to earthly things and become accepting of other people and life as you move into unconditional love.

As I look psychically at my clients, I can identify someone who is ready for the Fourth Initiation because they have a relatively clear aura. By this point the soul has been purifying the initiate by dropping more and more light in. Also there is a ball of light above the initiate, about four feet in diameter, which is the spirit. It will become much larger before it begins to move in at a higher initiation. Any darkness remaining in the aura occurs in patches, as opposed to general darkness everywhere. The dark areas represent attachments, past-life programs, and theme issues that will be cleared during Dark Night of the Soul. By the middle to late stages of the Fourth Initiation, the chakras have begun to break down and lose their cone shape. They begin to wobble and weaken as they lose density during the intense clearing process of the Dark Night.

Facilitating a Fourth Initiation Ceremony

A lot happens during this ceremony, usually more than with the Third Initiation. The Fourth Initiation ceremony can be approached in the same style and manner as the Third.

Begin by clearing anything that stands in the way, including any attachments to the material, mental, or emotional worlds. This does not mean they have to be completely gone from the initiate's life, but it does mean that he/she is aware of what the attachments are. In fact, after you have integrated this initiation, you can still keep most of the things that you enjoy on the physical plane, but you will no longer be attached to them. And when they are removed by the soul, you won't experience such loss because now you are able to view things from the witness position instead of feeling like a victim.

In the Fourth Initiation ceremony, place the person on a massage table, with sweet music and candles in a room that has been cleared previously (e.g., using sage or other clearing agents) to remove any negative energy. Take the initiate through the expansion process (described for the Third Initiation) to become as large as the universe. The masters, teachers, guides, and angels then take the initiate to the location of the ceremony, whether that is a heavenly palace or mountain meadow. Once the initiate is standing before God, God blesses the initiate by word, touch, or look, or simply as the Presence.

As soon as this portion of the ceremony is complete, the initiate will begin embodying the seven lower rays: red, blue, yellow, green, orange, indigo, and violet. The rays are sent into the crown chakra one after the other, not in any particular order. Each color has a different vibration, from dense to very subtle or light. It usually takes one to two minutes for each color to integrate into the physical body. You, the facilitator, and/or the initiate may shake or vibrate as each color integrates into all bodies, muscles, bones, and cells. It is very obvious when a color has been integrated because the shaking stops. Then the masters send the next layer of light in, until all of the rays have been integrated.

After the initiation ceremony, the initiate feels more connected to spirit. He/she also may have been given a preliminary understanding of his/her mission in this life.

FIFTH INITIATION

The Fifth Initiation is when the heart opens to begin receiving the Christ Consciousness. This is the opening to unconditional love. Once you have attuned with Christ Consciousness and become consciously aware of it, you can begin integrating more and more light and unconditional love. This is where you begin to move into timelessness, love, reverence, and joy. You begin to appreciate the magnitude of who you really are as a huge body of light.

With this initiation, you have embodied enough soul to comprehend that we all create every aspect of our reality by our thoughts and feelings. You begin to really comprehend that there are no accidents or coincidences. This involves reframing your understanding of creation at the higher levels, which is much more subtle (lighter in vibration), than third-dimensional experiencing, which is material, concrete. In fact, this is where you are shown how to reframe and restructure your future and your beliefs in the large scheme of All That Is. You begin to be in sync with creation and manifestation. You can then sit in the middle of it and watch it happen from the "witness" position.

In these accelerated times, the effect from our

thoughts and feelings can be immediate. Once you become aware of that, you are able to rethink your actions to create a different outcome. For example, when you smile at someone, you usually will receive a smile in return; when you scowl, this can create a scowl in return.

At the Fifth Initiation, God and the masters show initiates how powerful we really are and how to use this power to raise the vibration and consciousness of humankind for the sake of peace and unconditional love on planet Earth. This can be done consciously or through the dream state or in meditation.

When someone is ready for the Fifth Initiation, I begin to see the pink light (luminous dusty rose) of unconditional love in the person's aura. I also can feel the sweetness of the spirit. Sometimes I even smell a fragrance like roses. Prior to the initiation, I see Christ Consciousness in the antahkarana. At this stage, the antahkarana (the shaft of light that connects you with both Heaven and Earth) is very wide, about twice the size of the head. The Christ Consciousness appears as a luminous white light that vibrates in the antahkarana as it begins its descent downward. As soon as I see that light, I look at the heart. If I see a big, beautiful, open area with rays of light-pink and/or light green-coming out of the heart chakra, I can tell this person is in the process of developing unconditional love in preparation for the embodiment of the Christ Consciousness.

Prior to this initiation, you may be very fatigued because you have worked so hard at integrating the Fourth Initiation and going through all the Dark Night dramas. This exhaustion facilitates the continuing surrendering process. And even though you are tired, spirit feeds you enough energy to carry on. The ego has diminished greatly by this point. Your energy usually is more subtle than aggressive.

In the Fifth Initiation, your conscious awareness is becoming ever more vast. You are still frustrated, but usually continue to practice your disciplines such as meditation, contemplation, chanting, etc. This is nearing the end of clearing personality and soul issues, readying you for the higher consciousness and electrical energy of the spirit. Your body is now vibrating in the "500 megahertz" range and you are becoming lighter all the time. Most human bodies vibrate at about 45 to 65 megahertz. The higher the state, the higher the vibration.

FACILITATING A FIFTH INITIATION CEREMONY

I begin this initiation ceremony by helping the initiate to clear any issues that stand in the way of opening the heart. This can include past resentments, grudges, hostilities, etc. The initiate also must be cleared of anything that stands in the way of taking responsibility for his/her mission now. Even if the initiate doesn't know what the mission is, he/she must be open to it. As soon as the initiate has been cleared and is ready for the ceremony, have him/her lie on a massage table.

By this time in the initiation process, the initiate's consciousness is expanded enough that it is not necessary to do the expansion exercise detailed for the Third and Fourth Initiation ceremonies. Instead, have the initiate call forth the soul and spirit. The ceremony for this initiation is very nebulous. The initiate usually is taken before God. I feel rushes of energy coming through me and around the initiate.

In the last six months of 1999, Horus, the Egyptian God, began to step into my body from behind to lead this Fifth Initiation. There is not much I can say about how to facilitate this ceremony since the process is channeled through me and is individually tailored to the initiate's needs.

I have removed crystals and implants, done sound toning, and spoken in tongues. I do see specific masters showing up for the initiate to guide the process of opening the heart and connecting with the vibration of unconditional love. The Christed Self bridges soul and spirit, bringing them closer together. The presence of the masters is also an affirmation of the relationship between the master and the initiate. This confirms the level of mastery the initiate has achieved. What the initiate receives from the ceremony is a merger with the saints or masters to be pondered and contemplated each day. The initiate must always remember that he/she is never alone. The Spiritual Hierarchy/Great White Brotherhood and the spirit form a very unique and masterful relationship to be respected and honored by the initiate at all times.

SIXTH INITIATION

The Sixth Initiation is when the soul, the spirit, and the Christ Consciousness begin to merge and work together and be embodied. The Sixth Initiation begins the direct attunement to spirit. Spirit is the godself above the soul. It is also known as the Monad, or I AM Presence. Attunement to spirit means touching the spirit. This is where you find yourself touching the lower part of the spirit. Your aura has become large and resilient enough. You are now beginning a new process in your relationship with God, the universe, and the cosmos. This is the initiation of bliss, peace, and perfection.

The spirit is made up of all the many colors of the luminous higher rays. You previously housed the energy of the lower seven rays (colors) that were given to you at the Fourth Initiation. Therefore, your connection to the spirit is magnetic and the ray energy within you attracts the spirit.

You are magnetically pulled up to connect to spirit. You go up, barely touching the bottom part of the spirit, gather light magnetically, and pull it down into you to be integrated. Then you swiftly go back up again for more light. This filling of yourself with the sweet love from spirit is the reward you have been waiting for. At last you are consciously beginning to experience the love of God and feel that your hard work and devotion was worth it. After the attunement to spirit, you are operating in many different dimensions and planes, all at the same time.

Another part of the Sixth Initiation is the absorption of the soul. Before the Sixth Initiation you must have integrated almost all levels of the soul. Any remaining oversoul is illuminated and absorbed into spirit during the Sixth Initiation. At the completion of this absorption, all karma has been completed and you are self-realized.

In my opinion, your astrology changes in the Sixth Initiation after you have completely integrated the soul. Your astrological sign becomes that of your soul rather than of your ego-personality. Consequently, you transcend the astrological influences of your ego-level chart. The sign in your mid-heaven on your astrological chart IS the sign of your over soul.

During the integration of the Sixth Initiation your cells, bones, DNA, RNA, and everything that was the old self in the physical body is transmuted. The blueprint for the perfect Self is merging with you. This happens because the Sixth Initiation is a major boost to the development of the lightbody. The speed, of course, varies by individual, but it can be phenomenal. In one instance, a client had patches of the lightbody grid visible prior to the initiation; within two weeks following the initiation ceremony, her lightbody extended eight to ten feet around her body. This also seems to be the time when the energies start firing across both hemispheres of the brain. You gain better access to both your left and right-brained skills and begin using more of the brain.

You have been experiencing access to the Universal Mind since the Fourth Initiation. At the completion of the Sixth Initiation, with self-realization, you discard the Universal Mind and move into direct perception as you merge with the spirit in the higher initiations.

According to some sources, the Sixth Initiation, or possibly the Fifth, is when you can be shown how to manifest and dematerialize matter. However, such powers and gifts of magic must come from spirit rather than from ego. You must be clear enough, and unconditionally loving enough, to handle these powers benevolently before they are given to you.

The Sixth Initiation used to be called the Initiation of Ascension. At this point, Jesus ascended and left the planet. But, due to the increase of planetary energy, we now ascend at higher initiations. Of course, our spirits can choose for us to leave at this or any initiation if our mission on Earth is completed and we can serve better from the other side. However, the Spiritual Hierarchy currently is encouraging us to stay longer so we may serve for a longer period of time in a physical body in the new millenium.

You have become very clear at this stage. There is considerably less pain now because most shame has been released and you are rarely controlled by others' thoughts or feelings about you. You must release all emotional attachments; you are evaluated at this stage and, if you still have lower desire level attachments, you will be held here until purified.

I sometimes feel a tremendous pain in people at this point. Sixth is the final surrender of the ego. For someone who is still gripping and clutching onto something the ego wanted to attain in a physical body, such as success or money or true love, it is excruciatingly painful. The person realizes he/she is heading back to God and may never, ever, have what the ego wanted. The initiate must let go of that attachment or he/she can get stuck in that place indefinitely. The initiate must work through and clear the issue(s) and surrender to spirit and his/her place in the divine plan. The spirit plan may or may not include what the ego wanted. If it is included, then the initiate can have it, but must not be attached to it. This can happen only after the initiate releases the ego drive. This should be a time of final releasing of all attachments and addictions. Once this is accomplished, this initiation becomes the level of true happiness.

This is the stage of becoming bold as you feel more and more self-empowered. You have an understanding in this initiation that you are a spiritual master, always have been, and will continue to be throughout time. You learn to rely on your own inner voice, the voice of spirit. You become more intuitive and rarely need to go to an outside source for information. Most of your answers come from within. If you do need help, you are clearly and consciously directed to whatever or whomever you need. The greatest gift you can give yourself is to get out of the way and trust.

In the Sixth Initiation, your awareness becomes global. Some initiates expand enough that they can feel earthquakes and events happening on the other side of the world. Certain initiates are asked to step into place geographically to "ground" the overshadowing of the grid/perfect blueprint of the Earth. This is part of a process whereby the power centers on the planet are being activated. Certain initiates are relocated to these power spots at certain times of the year to help hold the light.

When someone is ready for the Sixth Initiation, I can tell that now he/she KNOWS. The initiate has moved into a position where he/she knows it is too late to turn back and has surrendered his/her life to God. I no longer see the vibrating light of the Christ Consciousness in the initiate's antahkarana because that was embodied during the Fifth Initiation. In fact, I no longer see the antahkarana at all. I am sure it is still there, but it has gotten so wide that I can't see the edges of it. It has become a part of the initiate and the initiate has become a part of it. The soul star has been in the heart since the Third Initiation, growing bigger and bigger all the time. By the Sixth Initiation, the soul star is huge and I see it as a beaming light that radiates out of the heart in all directions.

Following the Sixth Initiation ceremony and during the integration process, I no longer see the soul as a separate entity. The initiate is the soul. I also can see the spirit resting above the head like a huge ball of light. In size, it is eight to ten feet in diameter or larger. From this point on, the amount of spirit above the head becomes bigger and bigger. I have seen several self-realized beings with a spirit that was about twenty to fifty feet in diameter. With saints, I don't even see the borders of the aura anymore because they have become so vast. They are spirit.

The unified chakra, which has been forming since the late stages of the Fourth Initiation, forms completely in the Sixth Initiation. At the beginning of the Sixth Initiation, the chakras have almost completely broken down as they have lost density. The second and fifth chakras are usually the last to go. These are power chakras that deal with physical issues of relationships and communication.

I also see that the aura has changed to pink and green in color. The green is a luminous light green of the Christ Consciousness from the heart. The pink is the luminous dusty rose of unconditional love from the universe. The opening of this energy in the high heart affects all the glands, especially opening the pineal and pituitary because now you are changing chemically into light. The lightbody is really active, and the milky liquid protein that spirit is sending down into the cells is transmuting the cells into light. In the Sixth Initiation, all the landmarks that I have used - the soul, soul star, antahkarana, chakras, Christ Consciousness, and the forming lightbody grid - have merged together into the lightbody. You have become a unity of light.

Facilitating a Sixth Initiation Ceremony

As usual, I begin this ceremony by helping the initiate to clear any issues that stand in the way of receiving this powerful infusion of cosmic light. Much of the material that needs to be cleared involves past-life memories. Some of these memories involve previous attempts at ascension that resulted in failure and death. Once cleared, the initiate moves to a massage table. As with the Fifth Initiation, there is no need for the expansion process.

As I watch during the actual initiation ceremony, I see an alignment of the initiate and the creators and co-creators of the universe. The initiate sometimes is shown the plans for the planet and universe. In other words, he/she is given the map for the rest of the work to be done in this life. The theme for the new millennium is love, peace, and unity.

Many times the initiate is given a secret mantra or message to take home and use daily. As the facilitator, I sometimes am not able to hear this secret, or I may not be able to understand what it means.

The Sixth Initiation ceremony is sometimes facilitated by Horus. I am in an altered state, so I do not usually consciously remember the specifics of what happens. However, after talking with initiates about their experiences, several things usually happen:

- I run energy through the initiate's body to clear any blockages.

- I remove crystals that had prevented the lightbody from connecting to the cells of the body.
- I channel specific and personal information for the initiate, including the personal mantra and information about the mission.
- At some point the initiate goes before God and I assist in visualizing and interpreting the symbolic events being shown.
- Since this is the initiation where the soul is totally absorbed, the ceremony usually contains some clearing up of past life issues and/or receiving past-life information or gifts.
- I tone and/or speak in an ancient language(s). My sense is that these are words of a religious nature.
- I physically weave the lightbody into the physical level.
- I help to integrate the higher rays into the aura and body.

The Sixth Initiation is incredibly powerful. The energy of the higher rays and the spirit vibrate at such a high level that afterwards all involved experience physical shaking, heightened emotional sensitivity, visual distortions, and extrasensory perception (ESP).

Many people do this initiation ceremony during the dream- state or on the other side. Sometimes the initiation happens while the person is sleeping because the ego is silent. The person is lifted out of the body by spiritual masters and travels to the ascension temples. Many times people remember these initiations as dreams. Also, we can leave our bodies (as in death) and go through the initiation on the other side of the veil.

SEVENTH INITIATION AND ABOVE

The Seventh Initiation historically has been the last one that could be done while in the physical body. However, in these times of planetary ascension, it appears that more humans are reaching even higher levels while in the body. The Seventh, Eighth, and Ninth initiations are "Spirit Merge." This merging process is accomplished in three levels. The Tenth Initiation is "God Merge," or absorption into God.

With these higher initiations, you must be one hundred percent mission-oriented to even stay on the planet. You are part of the greater plan. You know when you will be leaving your body. And you have your work to do between now and then. By the Ninth Initiation, you have so little physical substance that you sometimes create physical problems to hold yourself into the body (e.g., broken bones, polyps, tumors). You are very detached from the dramas of the physical world. You are complete and full of unconditional love by the time you are "spirit-merged." You affect millions of people with your aura. No movement or act is without divine intent. The longing and the continuous searching for God are gone. You are pure consciousness and enlightened. You are at peace.

By the end of the Ninth Initiation, "spirit-merged" and "spirit-realized," you are the perfected Self. You burn with the sweetness of God. The solar kundalini (Holy Spirit) fills you due to your connection with spirit. Your lightbody connects with the electrical grid of the solar system and you become one with All That Is. You begin training for an office in the Spiritual Hierarchy. You have achieved mastership and are preparing to ascend.

As soon as you are able to have a clear, immediate vision of God, you are absorbed. This is the Tenth

Initiation. You are "God-realized" at this point. You then will be participating with and as God at this level. There are no more lifetimes incarnate on planet Earth, unless you knowingly choose to stay or to come back to serve. Few humans become clear enough to achieve this level.

Another form of ascension is instant dematerialization. This can only be done by the God Force from above. This can happen in the Tenth Initiation. There is an agreement between you and God to just vanish and step into an assignment on the other side.

The highly evolved people I have seen recommend being loving, living the Ten Commandments, and using spiritual practices such as meditation and/or contemplation. It is also important to laugh and have fun. Currently, there are only a few people at this level who are still living on the planet. Unfortunately, many of them are recluses and have very little association with humans anymore. We are not able to witness their demonstration of power. For the few who do allow us to be in their presence, this is always a true honor and gift.

ENLIGHTENMENT IS A PROCESS

Each initiation is a process of many levels that must be integrated; and each stage can last for months, years, or lifetimes. As you move through the initiations, you can find yourself moving up and down between two or three of them at a time. For example, you can be in the Fifth Initiation, which is love, and have an outburst of rage. But it will be short-lived, because you will be able to drop into your heart more readily and clear the emotion. Once cleared, you can return to the love state.

Please remember, this is a process. It takes time for all the old beliefs and ideas to be dissolved and removed;

and for the new ideas of wholeness, purpose, and love to be integrated. My personal experience of clearing issues, habits, and diseases has taken years. I gave up cigarettes in 1989, then began eliminating food addictions that caused migraines in the middle 1990s. Most recently, I have released the need for migraine medications since the migraines are gone. There are a few conditions I continue to heal, but considering the years of abuse I gave this body, an amazing amount of healing has taken place. The process is almost completed.

The major building of the lightbody seems to take place during the Sixth Initiation. However, the process begins with the Third Initiation or Soul Merge. In these spiritually accelerated times, more and more people are coming to me who have already started building their lightbody and are well into their Fourth Initiation, but they are unaware of this and think they are just starting on their spiritual path. It is happening faster and faster and the individual's consciousness is not keeping up. These people who think they are beginners have been on their path at least through the Third and part of the Fourth Initiation.

Many times with the people who are further along than they know, the lightbody grid is almost hidden. It is developing on the backside and is just starting to come around to the front. Immediately when I tell them what is happening and have them say the Unified Chakra Invocation (from *Lightbody* by Tashira Tachi-Ren), the grid starts forming in the front. I have sat and watched the lines of light connecting in the front and all over. The realization that they are in the process activates the lightbody formation. It moves rapidly. Sometimes it is so strong and building so fast that I can hardly see their faces because they have become so light.

I also see a lot of people who back out of the spiritual growth process sometime in the Third Initiation. They have seen how hard the Fourth can be and they decide not to do it. They choose to remain at the ego level and not give up their attachments to physicality. Some of these people come back. They live the third-dimensional life for ten years or so, then get serious again about their spiritual growth; or they drop out to have children and once the kids are grown they return actively to their spiritual path. Once people make a decision to continue on and they get into the Fourth Initiation, they usually have the resolve to stick with it.

I think that another major decision point comes in the Sixth Initiation. People have the choice to take their growth and not move further on the path of initiation; they are not seeking self-realization, spirit-realization, God-realization, or enlightenment. They choose to stay a human and live a human life. They may come back later, perhaps in the next lifetime. But since their awareness is high, they will go to a higher plane when they leave the body. When people die, they go to the level that their consciousness has attained. For most people this is either the astral/emotional plane or the causal/mental plane.

As you can see, ascension is an exciting, inspiring topic. Now is a wonderful time to have incarnated on planet Earth. My personal journey from darkness to light has been quite an adventure! The goal of enlightenment and ascension has given me the courage and incentive to continue growing and changing. The information and techniques in this book have helped me tremendously. In my work as a healer and spiritual counselor, I see these techniques helping many others as well. I hope that my story and this information will inspire and help you on your own spiritual journey. Enjoy!

Transforming Darkness into Light

BIBLIOGRAPHY

Bailey, Alice, and Tibetan Master, Djwhal Khul. *Ponder on This, A Compilation:* Lucis Publishing, 1971

Brennan, Barbara Ann. *Hands of Light:* Pleiades books, 1987

Castaneda, Carlos. *Tales of Power:* Pocket Books, re-issue 1992

Chidvilasanda, Swami. (Gurumayi) *My Lord Loves a Pure Heart:* A Siddha Yoga Production/The SYDA Foundation, 1994

Dass, Ram, and Stephen Levine. *Grist For The Mill:* Celestial Arts, 1988

Dass, Ram. *Be Here Now:* Crown Publishing, 1978

Disciples, Two. *The Rainbow Bridge II Link with the Soul-Purification:* Rainbow Bridge Productions, fourth edition 1994

Fortune, Dion. *Psychic Self-Defence:* The Aquarian Press, 1985

Fox, Emmet. *Sermon on the Mount:* Harper San Francisco, 1989

Hawkins M.D., David R. *Power vs. Force:* Veritas Publishing, 1995

Hurtak, J.J. *The Book of Knowledge, Keys of Enoch:* The Academy for Future Science. Fourth edition 1996

Linder, Jean Rita. *The Past Lives: Using Past Lives as a Tool for Transformation and Growth:* Publication in progress, 2000

McClure, Janet. *Prelude To Ascension: Tools for Transformation:* Light Technology Publications, 1996

Messenger, Charol. *The New Humanity, Our Destiny:* Xlibris Publishing, 2000

Muktananda, Swami, and Paul Zweig. *Play of Consciousness:* The SYDA Foundation

Peers, E. Allison. *Dark Night of the Soul, St. John of the Cross:* Doubleday Publishing, 1990

Sanella M.D., Lee. *The Kundalini Experience:* Psychosis or Transcendence: Integral Publishing, 1988

Strieber, Whitley. *Communion:* Avon Publishing, revised 1995

Stubbs, Tony. *The Ascension Handbook, Channeled Materials by Serapis:* republished, New Leaf Press, 1999

Tashira Tachi-ren, and Archangel Ariel. *What is Lightbody:* republished, New Leaf Press, 1999